Other volumes in The Concord Library
SERIES EDITOR: John Elder

*Eighty Acres: Elegy for a
Family Farm*
RONALD JAGER

Tarka the Otter
HENRY WILLIAMSON

The Insect World of J. Henri Fabre
EDWIN WAY TEALE, EDITOR

A Land
JACQUETTA HAWKES

In Limestone Country
SCOTT RUSSELL SANDERS

Nature and *Walking*
RALPH WALDO EMERSON
AND HENRY DAVID
THOREAU

Following the Bloom
DOUGLAS WHYNOTT

*Finding Home: Writing on Nature
and Culture from* Orion *Magazine*
PETER SAUER, EDITOR

*The Very Rich Hours: Travels in
Orkney, Belize, the Everglades,
and Greece*
EMILY HIESTAND

*Staying Put: Making a Home in a
Restless World*
SCOTT RUSSELL SANDERS

Thoreau on Birds
FRANCIS H. ALLEN, EDITOR

THE GEOGRAPHY OF
Childhood

THE GEOGRAPHY OF
Childhood

▲ ▲ ▲ ▲ ▲ ▲ ▲ ▲ ▲ ▲ ▲

WHY CHILDREN NEED WILD PLACES

Gary Paul Nabhan
Stephen Trimble

PHOTOGRAPHS BY
Stephen Trimble

BEACON PRESS
Boston

For
Dustin Corvus and Laura Rose Nabhan
and
Dory Elizabeth and Jacob Douglas Trimble

BEACON PRESS
25 Beacon Street
Boston, Massachusetts 02108-2892

Beacon Press Books
are published under the auspices of
the Unitarian Universalist Association of Congregations.

99 98 97   8 7 6 5

An earlier version of Trimble's "Sing Me Down the Mountain"
appeared in the "New Nature Writing" issue of *Witness*
(vol. III, no. 4, Winter, 1989) and again in *On Nature's Terms:
Contemporary Voices* (Texas A&M University Press, 1992).
Nabhan's early version of "Going Truant," called
"The Evolution of a Naturalist," first appeared in *Petroglyph*
(vol. 2, no. 1, Spring, 1990); another version appeared in
The Land Report from Salinas, Kansas, the same year.
Nabhan's "A Child's Sense of Wildness" was published first
in *Orion* (Fall, 1990); it appeared in *Northern Lights*
and in the *Arizona Daily Star* the same year,
and was later reprinted in *Finding Home*,
Peter Sauer, ed. (Beacon Press, 1992). An early version of
Trimble's "The Scripture of Maps" appeared in *Portland*,
the University of Portland magazine (Spring, 1993).

Text design by Janis Owens

Library of Congress Cataloging-in-Publication Data
Nabhan, Gary Paul.
The geography of childhood : why children need wild places / Gary
Paul Nabhan and Stephen Trimble ; photographs by Stephen Trimble.
p.   cm. — (The Concord library)
Includes bibliographical references.
ISBN 0-8070-8524-3 (cloth)
ISBN 0-8070-8525-1 (paper)
1. Nature—Psychological aspects. 2. Environment and children.
3. Child rearing. I. Trimble, Stephen. II. Title. III. Series.
BF353.5.N37N32 1994
155.4—dc20   93-31484

There was a child went forth every day,
And the first object he looked upon, that object he became,
And that object became part of him for the day or a certain part
  of the day,
Or for many years or stretching cycles of years.

Walt Whitman, "There Was a Child Went Forth,"
Leaves of Grass, written in 1855, published in 1871

. . . that was the main thing about kids then: we spent an awful lot of
time doing nothing. . . . All of us, for a long time, spent a long time
picking wild flowers. Catching tadpoles. Looking for arrowheads. Getting
our feet wet. Playing with mud. And sand. And water. You understand,
not doing anything. What there was to do with sand was let it run
through your fingers. What there was to do with mud was pat it, and
thrust in it, lift it up and throw it down. . . . My world, as a kid, was full
of things that grownups didn't care about.

Robert Paul Smith,
"Where did you go?" "Out." "What did you do?" "Nothing."
1957

. . . a ditch somewhere—or a creek, meadow, woodlot, or marsh. . . .
These are places of initiation, where the borders between ourselves and
other creatures break down, where the earth gets under our nails and a
sense of place gets under our skin.
  . . . Everybody has a ditch, or ought to. For only the ditches and
the fields, the woods, the ravines—can teach us to care enough for all
the land.

Robert Michael Pyle, *The Thunder Tree*, 1993

Contents

▲ ▲ ▲ ▲ ▲ ▲ ▲ ▲

Preface

▲　▲　▲　▲　▲　▲　▲　▲　▲　▲

The geography and natural history of childhood begins in family, at home, whether that home is in a remote place or in a city. Many naturalists start their journeys on ditchbanks, in empty lots—in any open space just beyond the backyard fence. In our essays here, we consider the influences that natural settings, native plants, and wild animals have on toddlers and teenagers; on girls as well as boys; on families and community traditions; and on a variety of cultures, not just those characterized as "the Western World." Simply put, we are concerned about how few children now grow up incorporating plants, animals, and places into their sense of *home*.

Over the last several decades, most published writing about the human quest for contact with the natural world can be classified as "outdoor adventure literature." This genre has focused on the exploits of lone individuals or small groups of Anglo-Americans, usually well-educated urban males between the ages of twenty and forty, seeking recreational pleasures in remote and sometimes formidable wilderness areas. Indeed, when the two of us met twenty years ago, we were the typical young white males bent on being scientist-explorers in the far reaches of the earth.

We shared our first tentative dialogue in 1973, in the Miami International Airport in the middle of the night, where we were to rendezvous with other students joining a field science course bound for Ecuador and the Galápagos Islands. Within a few minutes, we discovered a remarkable number of shared interests and mutual friends. Once in Guayaquil, our group booked passage to the islands on the only available ship—the *Cristobal Carrier*, a broken-down freighter with a drunken captain straight out of Conrad. Bunks shortened toward the stern, and, since we were the two shortest males aboard, we were assigned the last cabin on the men's side of the ship.

In the years that followed, our friendship has grown beyond outdoor adventures, although we still greatly value the time we can be in wild country together. We have come to know each other's families and colleagues, edited each other's work, interviewed one another for publication, and exchanged many ideas on nature and culture. Now, after two decades of friendship, each of us has become the father of two children and the author of several books.

In 1990, we realized that we both had published essays that centered on how our children's relationships to the natural world had begun to change our own. We both hoped to give our children strong and satisfying connections to nature, and we wondered how best to help them make those connections with places and organisms that had not been engineered solely to meet our utilitarian needs.

In watching the strong emotional reactions of audiences hearing these essays read aloud, we realized that we had struck a chord—perhaps because they elicited such vivid childhood memories of contact with wild nature among the listeners. It was then that we decided to collect under one cover a series of complementary essays about children and the natural world. This book is the result.

Being neither educators nor environmental therapists, we have few prescriptions to offer parents and classroom teachers. This is not a guide to environmental education nor to "green" child-raising. Rather, it is an exchange of ideas, images, and stories between two natural historians who are finding their way as fathers while they watch their own children's behavior in the wild unfold. For guidance, we look to our own childhoods, to our children, and to children of other places and cultures with whom we have spent time. We find enormous diversity in these lives, but we also sense some common ways in which wildness— even in its simplest forms—can nourish a lasting attachment to the earth, and, in turn, nurture self-esteem.

We know, too, that many now consider children's experience of wildness a luxury rather than a basic human need. Many young people, both in the United States and in less affluent countries, have no time to familiarize themselves with the names of the few plants and animals that remain in their immediate surroundings, because they are busy absorbing other taxonomies they believe more critical to their daily survival. Consider a PBS interview conducted in the wake of the Los Angeles riots of 1992. One adolescent in south-central L.A. listed a half-dozen different automatic weapons used on the streets, and he was able to identify each by its sound. He did not see this as an unusual piece of discriminatory knowledge for someone his age. These were the sounds he heard, learned, and sensed to be vital to his own existence. In another place and time, he would have spoken as matter-of-factly about the calls of six common species of hawks and owls.

Children *do* need wildness, and in this book we spiral around that premise like moths coming to an open, nectar-laden flower. Our spiral dance may lead you on a passage through many questions—and some questions may resist immediate resolution. But in the questioning lies the key: a heightened awareness of the primacy of these issues, with each parent and youngster asking their questions in uniquely personal ways. We hope our book will help you to frame new questions, to see old questions with fresh perspectives, and invent new responses for both.

During the last few years, both of us have received considerable stimulation and encouragement during meetings with nature writers, scholars, educators, and editors associated with the Orion Society, in rendezvous at Glen Brook, Cape Cod, Camp Tontozona, Williams College, and elsewhere. We have been particularly inspired by the words of our colleagues Franklin Burroughs, Robert Finch, John Hay, Nan Jenks Jay, Richard Nelson, Robert Michael Pyle, Sara St. Antoine, Peter Steinhart, Deanne Urmy, and Terry Tempest Williams during these get-togethers. We are grateful to Deanne, and to our agent, Tim Schaffner, for helping us to develop our mutual interest into this collaborative book project.

GARY PAUL NABHAN
STEPHEN TRIMBLE

Acknowledgments

I am grateful to have had this opportunity for protracted dialogue with Steve Trimble, who is among the steadiest of friends and finest parents I have encountered during my life. Together with his wife, Joanne Slotnik, and my wife, Caroline Coalter Wilson, we have the chance to discuss our own responsibilities in guiding children in their encounters with natural surroundings, and to discover the limitations to our more naive assumptions about this process. I must also acknowledge that my own children have benefited from role models other than the ones Caroline and I fill while we are taking them camping, hiking, and exploring wild places. Karen Reichhardt, Susan Kunz, Eric Mellink, Humberto Suzan, Guadalupe Malda, Culver Cassa, Terry Tempest Williams, Wade Sherbrooke, Sara St. Antoine, and many others have offered my children unique perspectives to fuel their fascination with flora and fauna. Jerri and Chuck Buxton have also been anchors.

A number of my own teachers and mentors, including James Mason, Dorothy Ives, and Curtis McCray (and through him, Paul Shepard) have greatly influenced my thinking about the learning process and environments in which such a process flourishes. In particular, Mason's direction of Wilder Forest and Pleasant Valley Farm has shaped my views of multicultural environmental education in informal settings. Jim Mason not only read portions of the manuscript, but introduced me to the fine work of Kamau Kambui, and to the *Children's Environments Quarterly*, the richest source of academic literature on children's responses to natural and artificial settings. Rosilda Manuel and Danny Lopez, two Tohono O'odham educators, Felipe Molina of Yoeme Pueblo, Clare and Bob Burton of Vision Quest, Willie Williams of NOLS, and Carol Cochran of the Arizona-Sonora Desert Museum also provided leads and comments. Particular thanks go to David Hancocks, Director of the Arizona-Sonora Desert Museum, who offered me an office, writer-in-residence status with the Museum's Education Department, and personal comments on manuscript chapters while in development. The Pew Scholars Program provided me with time and the opportunity to involve Sara St. Antoine, a graduate student at the Yale School of Forestry and Environmental Studies, as a collaborator in background research with Sonoran Desert children during the summer of 1992. Sara served not only as a sounding-board for my own ideas, but offered many creative insights of her own in a consistently cheerful and enthusiastic manner.

In the final stages of my drafts, I had the gift of being asked to participate in a retreat called "Testing the Biophilia Hypothesis" in Wood's Hole, Massachusetts. Organized by Steve Kellert and E. O. Wilson—both of whom had already influenced my ideas— this retreat gave me the chance to exchange ideas with a number of scholars who have considered the evolutionary basis for our affinity with other lifeforms. In particular, Paul Shepard, Flo Krall, David Orr, David Abrams, Richard Nelson, Gordon Orians, Judith Heerwagen, Aaron Katcher, Roger Ulrich, and Michael Soulé provided perspectives that allowed me to revise the chapter drafts one last time. I am grateful to them, and to Aina Niemela, Tom Lyon, and Peter Sauer, editors of earlier versions of these chapters that found their way into print at *Orion* magazine, *Petroglyph* magazine, *Northern Lights* journal, *The Land*

Report, and the Beacon Press anthology of *Orion* articles, *Finding Home*.

Lastly, my deepest thanks to Corvus and Thorny Desert Rose for having the good humor to tolerate and kid their papa when he was observing their natural history. I hope they'll write about why papas need wildness some day.

G.P.N.

My largest thanks go to Gary Nabhan, for his longtime friendship and encouragement and for suggesting that I join him in the adventure of this book. I have learned much in the writing and researching of it, but I have learned few ironclad rules for child-raising. I have wished that my children were five years older than they are, so I could tell more stories about them. But I suspect that even with those additional years of grappling with the issues we address here, I would not understand them fully. Parenting is the most challenging task I have faced, and as its challenges change daily, sometimes hourly, we all race to keep pace.

I am grateful to share this enormous adventure of child-raising with my wife, Joanne Slotnik. I also treasure Joanne's fierce editing; she demands that I have something to say and then say it clearly. I thank her for her clear-sightedness and honesty.

Joanne and Sharon Solomon reacted strongly to early drafts of these pieces, startling me with my naïveté regarding gender issues. Their comments led to my essay focusing on gender. Thanks to Tom Lyon and Brian Doyle, who edited earlier versions of two chapters for *Witness* and *Portland* magazines. Other helpful critiques on one or more essays came from: Barbara Berry, Marcia Bonta, Alan and Dolly Carroll, Dana Carroll, Theresa Cryns, Tara Curry, Jennifer Owings Dewey, Linda and

Carolyn Dufurrena, Teresa Jordan, Amy Kaplan, Tom Melton, Pat Musick, Jack Newell, Barbara Slotnik, Bea Slotnik, Chuck and Judy Smith, Lynne Tempest, and Ann Zwinger. Terry Tempest Williams, especially, helped me to reorganize my thinking in important ways. Deanne Urmy's editorial counsel was consistently wise. Many other friends discussed their childhoods and told stories and anecdotes, which I shamelessly stole for use here. Thanks to all of them for their generosity.

For help with my research in the rural West, I thank: the Dufurrenas of Denio, Nevada; in Ruby Valley, Nevada, the teachers and students at Ruby Valley School and Rod McQueary; and, in Twin Bridges, Montana, Dolly and Alan Carroll and the staff and students of Twin Bridges Elementary School. Linda and Carolyn Dufurrena run several field trips for small groups each year in the mountains surrounding their northern Nevada ranch; write to Dufurrena & Dufurrena Adventures, Star Route 397, Winnemucca, Nevada 89445.

In Salt Lake City: Abby Trujillo Maestas, executive director of the Rape Crisis Center, guided me with statistics and perspective on sexual violence; Jack Newell enthusiastically shared his knowledge of Deep Springs College; and Brant Calkin provided good leads. As always, Nora Naranjo-Morse of Santa Clara Pueblo, New Mexico, guided me toward a better understanding of Pueblo people.

I make clear in these essays my debt to my parents. From my father, Don Trimble, I learned to pay attention to the land. From my mother, Isabelle Trimble, I learned to be curious about people. I realized not long ago that, when asked about the nature of my religious training, the appropriate answer is: "My mother is Jewish, and my father is a geologist." In a confusing world, my father's assumption that landscape can orient stayed with me. "Geology"—nature, wildness, and the earth—laced with a Jew's value of family, learning, and ritual, is making a workable faith, and these values learned from my parents underlie what I write here.

Any remaining blunders and naïvetés are my own.

S.T.

Introduction

▲ ▲ ▲ ▲ ▲ ▲ ▲ ▲ ▲

Twenty years ago, in the early 1970s, I was spending a lot of time in a Boston ghetto, talking with children whose prospects for a comfortable life were exceedingly limited, if not grim. I had worked in the South during the 1960s, studied school desegregation as it took place in cities such as New Orleans and Atlanta, sometimes amidst great violence. Now I was back home, hearing about the constraints (or worse) of the North—the way black children, born to feel vulnerable and melancholic, struggle hard, even if the laws don't force upon them the kind of segregation so prevalent throughout the South. By then I had heard those Yankee children talk not only about race and class (in their own way, of course) but about other matters as well: their wishes for themselves, their doubts and fears, their daydreams, and not rarely their nightmares. In the South many urban children were born in the countryside and still had kin there, and so I was not surprised to hear both black and white children, living in the crowded city streets of, say, New Orleans, evoke another kind of life, which they sorely missed. But up North, many boys and girls have never really seen the countryside, nor have their parents, nor their grandparents.

Still, in 1974, I heard this from a twelve-year-old black girl who had been bussed to a previously all-white Boston school: "I guess I'm doin' all right. I'm studyin', and, like the teacher says, it pays off. A lot of time, though, I wish I could walk out of that school and find myself a place where there are no whites, no black folk, no people of any kind! I mean, a place where I'd be able to sit still and get my head together; a place where I could walk and walk, and I'd be walking on grass, not cement, with glass and garbage around; a place where there'd be the sky and the sun, and then the moon and all those stars. At night, sometimes, when I get to feeling real low, I'll climb up the stairs to our roof [she lived in a triple-decker building with a flat roof], and I'll look at the sky, and I'll say, hello there, you moon and all your babies—stars! I'm being silly, I know, but up there, I feel I can stop and think about what's happening to me—it's the only place I can, the only place."

There was more, much more—a city girl's evocation of a natural world she both yearned to know, yet hasn't come to know. She is not, thereby, responding to anyone's romanticism—nature as a kind of heaven. She is not hearkening back to past experiences in a countryside setting—using memory as an alternative to a contemporary time of turmoil and danger. She has not watched television programs or read books that tell her about the great glories of this or that rural landscape. Rather, she is responding to her own eyes, to her mind's imaginative search, at once a psychological and a moral one: the ardent desire of a city youth for a place, a space, that will connect her to land, to the air, to the sky, and to the world it holds—all of which, she senses in her bones, rather than thinks in her head, will give her, yes, back to herself. "If I was there [in the place she had conjured up], I'd be able to talk the way I want, and I'd hear myself, because there wouldn't be a lot of people listening and telling me what I said or what I should be saying."

I thought of her, of the passionate flight of fancy she had constructed, as I read *The Geography of Childhood*—of a child's earnest effort to find a place, a home of sorts that would be welcoming, refreshing, that would return her to her very humanity as the creature who looks at the world and wonders those utterly existentialist questions: Who are we? and where do we come from? and where are we headed? questions she far preferred to those being posed for her in a crowded, strife-torn school and neighborhood. It is the great gift of this book—so vivid and lyrical in its narrative presentation—that we are brought close, indeed, to an understanding of what that city girl tried to find for herself, what all of us want and need to discover: a connection with the universe itself in all its various elements.

In the pages that follow, two wise, knowing naturalists give us a glimpse of what children are and what they urgently need. Like us who are older, boys and girls want to take stock of things, try to make sense of them, and so doing, hunger to find a place where such moral introspection can occur with grace and dignity. The "geography" boys and girls ultimately want to explore and comprehend is that of life itself—its enormous range, its astonishing complexity, the many stories, of sorts, it has to tell us; and it is such a "geography" that the reader of this compelling, suggestive book will soon enough encounter—an original glimpse, most certainly, of our children as very much a part of what gets called the environment. All young people ache for nature in the way that Boston girl of a tenement house did, ache for nature as a part of their bread and water, their creaturely sustenance—and in these pages we get to know in thoughtful detail the depth and extent of that yearning, that aspect of childhood.

ROBERT COLES

A Child's Sense
of Wildness

*C*all it the boonies, the tules, the woods, the outback, the bush, the wilds, scrubland, hard scrabble, or just plain *country*. Whenever we've gone to play in the rough-and-tumble lands beyond the metropolitan grid, my children have taught me things that I never would have learned if we had hung around the house. It's true, the children might have been able to offer me insights about the world if we had stayed at home, but my guess is that I would have been less likely to notice and embrace them there. That's because too often I've assumed that the kids and I agree on all there is to know about the place where we routinely eat, wash, and sleep, *as if* they and I occupy and make sense out of the same familiar world.

We do not.

We sooner or later realize how differently each of us moves through any terrain. Going out together to discover new places is the surest way to be reminded that we do not see the land with the same eyes, nor smell it with the same nose. It sings different songs to each of us, and what we hear changes in accordance with our years.

I should have sensed such differences in perception during the weeks just prior to our family's summer camping trip. The kids seemed somewhat bored by the photo previews of parks we might see, and by the litany of place-names sung into their ears during our packing and preparation.

My children—Dustin Corvus, then seven going on fifteen, and Laura Rose, pushing age five—were born, raised, and baptized in the solar fire and cactus-stippled basins of the Sonoran Desert. Lumpy granite and low volcanic ranges had always rimmed their horizons. Little did they know what lay ahead of them in the geological jumble of northern Arizona and southern Utah: "more hills, holes, humps and hollows, reefs, folds, salt domes, swells and grabens, buttes, benches and mesas, synclines, monoclines and anticlines than you can ever hope to see and explore in one lifetime," that childlike mortal Edward Abbey once suggested. Little did I know what my children would allow me to see: Lilliputian landscapes often overlooked by educated adults seeking the Big Picture.

We were off, headed north for the canyon country of the Colorado Plateau, my mind set on our destination, Dustin's dwelling on what was immediately around us. As we worked our way through the Phoenix traffic jams, he became preoccupied with the omnivorous earth-movers cruising along outside his window. All sorts of heavy equipment were reshaping the land surrounding the new multi-storied office complex of the Salt River Project, the dam-and-ditch bureaucracy that controls where water flows in our stretch of the desert.

Dustin finally felt moved to speak out. "Papa, I don't like what they're doing. Scraping up all the dirt like that. They're taking more and more of the earth away until pretty soon it will be so small that we'll all be bumping into one another."

He shook his head sadly, then selected a Smokey the Bear propaganda piece from the pile of comic books and field guides we had brought along. He perused the comics between conversations with his sister, who spent much of the car time on this trip dressing her bears for the cooler climes we would find at higher elevations. About an hour and a half past Phoenix, as we rose in elevation from desert to pine forest, Dusty once more turned his attention to the world outside his window.

"Papa, where are we now?"

"Looks like we're coming into Coconino National Forest," I replied. "We'll be in forest more or less 'til dark, I guess."

Minutes passed.

"Are we coming into a city? I thought you said we would be in the forest until dark."

"Well, this is Flagstaff. It's grown up in the middle of Coconino National Forest. We'll be getting back into pine forests pretty soon."

He glanced out at the sluggish traffic along muddy roads under construction, the enormous but empty parking lots around new shopping malls, and the raw logs piled high along the railroad tracks.

"Papa," he asked tentatively, "when they cut the forest down to make a city, what do the forest rangers do then? Do they become police?"

The worried queries stopped once the camping began. During the following eight days, Dustin and Laura Rose seldom strayed more than eighty yards from our campsites. They found sagebrush leaves and juniper berries nearby and began to make perfumes by mashing the aromatic plant matter in their metal cups. While fetching water from little rivulets, they noticed the darting of water striders, the shapes of creek-washed stones. They scrambled up slopes to inspect petroglyphs and down arroyos to enter keyhole canyons.

We would rendezvous with others now and then, and that is when I realized how much time adults spend scanning the land for picturesque panoramas and scenic overlooks. While the kids were on their hands and knees, engaged with what was immediately before them, we adults traveled by abstraction. We often had in mind finding one of those classic "photo opportunities," a vantage over burnt orange and buff sandstone walls juxtaposed with cliff tops of mauve shales. We would position ourselves to peer out over a precipice, trying to count how many ridgelines there were between us and the far horizon. Whenever we arrived at such a promontory, Dustin and Laura Rose would approach it with me, then abruptly release their hands from mine, to scour the ground for bones, pine cones, sparkly sandstone, feathers, or wildflowers.

Long after the trip, I was reminded again that Dustin's attention had hardly ever turned to the oversized scenes. When we opened up a packet of his snapshots from the trip, we were greeted with crisp close-ups of sagebrush lizards, yuccas, rock art, and sister's funny faces. The few obligatory views of expansive canyons seemed, by contrast, blurred and poorly framed.

I have recently noticed this same phenomenon whenever I have encouraged the kids to go hiking by themselves around our Sonoran Desert home. "Don't go farther than the ridgeline," I'll caution, pointing to the volcanic crest a quarter-mile away. "You'll be able to see the house from there, and maybe some deer grazing in the next valley over . . ." Laura and Dusty will dutifully gather their gear—canteens, Fig Newtons, and self-assembled survival kits—then wander away from the house for a couple hours. While I water the garden or restack the firewood, I'll occasionally glance up to the rim to see if I can locate them.

Most frequently, however, I'll later hear them burst out of the brush across the road from the house, where a densely vegetated wash meanders not fifty yards away.

"Papa!" Laura cries. "Come over and see the hideout we made beneath a tree over there. See if you can walk down the wash and find us. I bet you won't even be able to figure out where we are!"

She takes my hand, leads me to the wash, makes me close my eyes, until both yell "Ready!" I proceed down the open gravel bed until I hear giggling coming from a concealed corner where a hackberry tree's canopy sweeps down to touch the ground. They have decorated a small opening with a wreath of wildflowers, and have made stools of pieces of wood found nearby.

"Let's see if you can fit in too, Papa," Laura suggests. "We've found the perfect place for eating cookies."

Over time, I've come to realize that a few intimate places mean more to my children, and to others, than all the glorious panoramas I could ever show them. Because I sense their comfort there, their tiny hand-shaped shelter has come to epitomize true intimacy for me. When my children are not staying with me, I often walk near their hide-away within the hackberry canopy, and imagine that they are simply nestled within it, not far away.

Gaston Bachelard once observed that "when we discover a nest, it takes us back to our childhood or, rather, to *a childhood*; to the childhoods we should have had . . . the nest image is generally childish." Bachelard is speaking an emotion deeper than nostalgia. He is touching upon a more ancient animal notion encoded within us: the simple comfort of the nest. "Physically, the creature endowed with a sense of refuge huddles up to itself, takes cover, hides away, lies snug, concealed. If we were to look among the wealth of our vocabulary for verbs that express the dynamics of retreat, we should find images based on animal movements of withdrawal, movements engraved within our muscles."

In retrospect, it is amusing to me that when I wished my children to have contact with wildness, I sent them "out," to climb high upon ridges and to absorb the grand vistas. Yet when they wished to gain a sense of wildness, of animal comfort, they chose not the large, but the small. In doing so, they may have been selecting a primordial connection with the earth and its verdant cover.

Environmental psychologist Mary Ann Kirkby has confirmed that most preschool children have a predilection for playing in nestlike refuges whenever such microhabitats are available. By mapping the behavior of twenty-six preschoolers on a half-acre playground, she found that they spent over half their time in three small refuges that covered only a tenth of the area accessible to them. A quarter of their time was spent acting out dramas under the cover of two densely vegetated areas on the margins of the playground. When they were not nestled beneath birches, dogwoods, junipers, and Scotch brooms, the children spent another quarter of their time on two elevated decks. Each deck was enclosed by widely spaced boards which allowed "lookouts" to scan the barren surroundings for potential "predators."

When Kirkby asked one four-year-old why he preferred such hiding spots with small openings, he replied, "Because I would need to see if you were coming." Probed further about why it was important to have a peephole for seeing out from his protected place, the boy responded matter-of-factly, "Because there might be wolves out there." Some psychologists now believe that such a predilection for enclosed spaces with good vistas is a genetically programmed human response, not merely the casual preference of a few children.

Kirkby believes too that there is some developmental basis for the way toddlers take refuge in natural and simply constructed, concealed settings. Such refuges extend the sphere of safety that children sensed earlier while still within the constant parental care they knew during their postnatal development.

It is a loss, then, that so many playgrounds have become dominated by machinelike recreational equipment, structured games, and paved-over areas. According to child psychologist Brian

Sutton-Smith, play has become too domesticated and regimented while playgrounds themselves have become more and more barren. Many today are devoid of vegetation with which to form nests, shelters, wands, dolls, or other playthings. He reminds us that "children's playground concerns also involve their sense of territory, boundaries, walls, apparatus, and surfaces." These concerns are best explored in a heterogeneous habitat, where several secret niches are harbored, the kinds that can no longer be found on prefabricated metal and plastic jungle gyms.

To counter the historic trend toward the loss of wildness where children play, it is clear that we need to find ways to let children roam beyond the pavement, to gain access to vegetation and earth that allows them to tunnel, climb, or even fall. And because formal playgrounds are the only outdoors that many children experience anymore, should we be paying more attention to planting, and less to building on them? Naturalist Franklin Burroughs is among those who have argued that children need places where they can roughhouse on tree limbs and swing on vines without being told that the plants are hands-off: "Better to let kids be a hazard to nature," Burroughs told a gathering of conservationists, "and let nature be a hazard to them."

After years of studying children's play, Sutton-Smith agrees. He would like to see kids have more "smells, tastes, splinters and accidents."

All this may be said to add up to how children get a political and cultural education that allows them to be members of the tribe of children. . . . [G]iven that it has long been known that children up until about 7 years of age communicate with each other more adequately by play than in speech, an argument can certainly be made that their childhood right to play is the same as our adult First Amendment right to free speech.

And if such an unalienable right to play requires appropriately wild settings in which to roost and express itself, we may well wonder whether we have depleted much of the habitat for learning and sensual intimacy from our children's lives.

Driving back through Phoenix near the end of our trip, I looked at its barrios, ghettos, tract house subdivisions, and trailer courts in a different light. There are vital young people in each of those residential areas, youngsters who may have wonderful imaginations, caring families, and great physical energy. Their lives may be rich socially, but are they given the range of environments in which to express themselves, to express the variety of human talents and emotions that are part of our genetic inheritance from having evolved in wild environments? Do the kids in garbage-strewn alleys making forts out of giant cardboard boxes gain the same pleasures as those who nestle within hollows formed by shrubbery, replete with the songs of cicadas and the smells of fragrant wildflowers?

I frankly don't know. Perhaps the core of each of those experiences is the same, and the indefatigable inventiveness of children can make the cardboard carton into as much of a nest as is needed. To be sure, children who do grow up in contact with wildlands have no hold on imaginative play; to suggest so would be subtly to reinforce the elitism that encourages the wealthier classes to escape out to the "undisturbed" edges of metropolitan areas so their children can have all the necessary "opportunities." That children *can* play creatively with only a cardboard box though is certainly no excuse to argue that inner-city kids need no more than what they have now.

As we all know, whether by default or by design, the poor have been left to fend with the rotting cores of our cities. In 1900, only 10 percent of the human population lived in cities of one million people or more. By the year 2000, 38 percent of the world population will be urbanized in such metropolitan areas where wildness has been severely impoverished. Of course, urban parks, backyards, and even abandoned railroad yards still offer some children the chance to romp and rummage, to seek out crawl spaces, hideaways, treehouses, and shrubby shelters. Nevertheless, an increasingly large proportion of inner-city children will never gain adequate access to unpeopled places, neither food-producing fields nor wildlands. They will grow up in a world where asphalt, concrete, and plaster cover more ground than shade-providing shrubs and their resident songbirds.

Consider that 57 percent of all children born this decade in developing countries will grow up in urban slums. A quarter of the children born in the United States in this next generation will start their lives in such slums, and it is predicted that most of these will never experience the lands upon which their food is grown, let alone terrains dominated by species other than our own. Should they have contact with other creatures, it will most likely be with the dogs, cats, cockroaches, starlings, and trees-of-heaven that have had much of the wildness drained out of them as they have adapted to human habitations. These children will grow up without nature as their measure because the environments they inhabit with be largely those of human (adult) design.

Call them habitats shaped by and for only one species. That, perhaps, is the most profound difference between wildlands and anthropogenic environments such as cities. The latter are not even *designed* to be habitable for other species, so that the weeds or English sparrows or Norway rats we find there survive despite our efforts to eradicate them.

Late in the canyon country journey with Dustin and Laura, I could not resist asking them how they thought cities were different from wild places. At age five, Laura simply rolled her eyes at such a question, and skipped away, to find a good place in the rocks for her bears to use as a dressing room. Dustin was a bit more tolerant of my query.

"Do you mean wilderness? Wilderness, I guess," Dustin sighed, "is full of plants and animals and rocks."

"Well," I replied, in a tone that only a father would try, "so is the botanical garden where I work. So is the zoo. What's the difference with wilderness?"

"Wilderness is where there are no roads. It is not caged-in," and then he added, as he left to go where his sister was exploring nooks and crannies in the sandstone, "it is not surrounded by chickenwire."

Dustin had offered me an interesting constellation of traits with which to contrast cities and wild places. Wilderness, as he called it, is *full* of things, of other lives, animal, vegetable and mineral. It has few inroads, so cannot be as easily dominated by human presence as can cities. Yet it is not easily circumscribed, not conveniently fenced to keep its wildness within or away from us. And from the ways Laura and Dusty behaved while we were in the canyon country, wilderness is not some scenic backdrop to gaze at; it is responsive to our exploratory urges. It is where you can play with abandon. In a word, *playfulness* may be the essence of wilderness experience.

It is too early to tell how long such a sense of wildness will stay with Dustin and Laura Rose. But there was a telling moment near the end of our trip, when I realized that such a sensibility can remain with people for the rest of their lives. Julie and Caroline Wilson are the daughters of Bates and Edie Wilson, who for many years hosted the motley crews of desert rats, photographers, cowboys, writers, and conservationists hooked on camping in Utah's canyon country. Bates, as superintendent at Arches National Monument (now Arches National Park), played a pivotal role in the creation of Canyonlands National Park. The Wilson girls went with their father, mother, and their friends on many a memorable jeep trip through that country, but also put in considerable time back behind a small rock house in Arches, when Bates was gone on less glamorous excursions. From the side door of their little home, they were but one hop, skip, and a jump away from slickrock benches, bluffs, cliffs, slopes, and *tinajas* which conformed to no human blueprint.

The girls would spend hours, alone or together, "back in the rocks," acting out dramas, staging dances, mounting expeditions, or watching clouds roll by. A little over a quarter century later, they escorted my children through their fantasyland, pointing out the Indian Cave, the Penguins, the Ballroom, the Princess's Bedroom, the Train, the Deer Pond. The scale of these little puddles, niches, crawl spaces, shelters, and passages fit Laura and Dustin to a tee.

"The smoothness of the rock is what attracts kids," Caroline offered. "You can scoot up and down it without scraping yourself."

We spent a morning scrambling on the slopes behind the former Wilson home. Side-stepping our way through a narrow passage at one point, Caroline rubbed up against a shrub, and stopped. She crushed a few leaves from a big sagebrush in her hands. "That smell!" she cried. "It's the one I grew up with, the one that means home to me!" A few minutes later, the bruised leaves of wild rosemary mint gave her much the same welcome.

Caroline still lives in the boonies, or *monte*, as her Sonoran neighbors call the wildlands of Organ Pipe Cactus National Monument, where she has worked as ranger-interpreter for the National Park Service. Her sister Julie is a physical therapist who calls the *malpais* of Tuba City, Arizona, her home. Both still car-camp, backpack, hillclimb, and riverrun whenever their work schedules permit. And their time in camps and canyons seems to have lent them a healthy perspective about humankind: a fondness for outdoor reunions with old friends, a willingness to greet and share stories with other hikers and backpackers passing by. These traits, I guess, were developed during the years of jeep rides and campouts that Bates and Edie would host in Canyonlands, but they also stem from the confidence the girls gained themselves while exploring the terrain behind their house in Arches. Ultimately, their social graces are not unrelated to their feeling at home in the wild.

There was a moment on the tour of their childhood playground that stands out above all others. Caroline led Laura and Dustin into the Ballroom, a slightly sloping bench of creamy Navajo sandstone overlooking the rock house. It was surrounded by nearly animate rockforms and a dozen floral fragrances. "This, Laura Rose," Caroline exclaimed, "this is where we danced!" She shut her eyes. Then, feeling the tilt of the sandstone beneath her feet, Caroline spun around and danced us up an image that she had carried with her from childhood.

"I *remember* these rocks!" Caroline whispered, somewhat astonished by the sudden upwelling of tears in her eyes. "They are as familiar to me as the freckles on my arm . . ."

I glanced down at Laura Rose, at my side. Her eyes grew wide. I closed mine and hoped that I would be around one day when, as a fully grown woman, Laura Rose will dance herself in place.

G.P.N.

The Scripture of Maps,
the Names of Trees

ever Summer Range, Snowy Range, Wind River
Range, Horse Heaven Hills. Rabbit Ears Pass, Togwo-
tee Pass, Lolo Pass, Chinook Pass. Longs Peak, Pikes
Peak, Grand Teton, Mount Rainier. Some people remember from
childhood the names of cherished baseball or football players.
Others can recite still the multisyllabic names of molded plastic
dinosaurs. My own remembered litany consists of place-names.

"Stevie, where do we turn?" my father would ask as I stared at
the land charted in the folds of paper on my lap. My father, of
course, knew which road to take at the next town. He also knew
that I loved being trusted to help find our way.

During my childhood in the fifties and sixties, the best high-
way maps of the western states came from Chevron stations, in
places like Rawlins, Wyoming, and Pendleton, Oregon. Stacked
in wire racks coated with dust cemented in automotive grease,
the maps waited for discovery, state by state. Down the road, I
studied the air-brushed mountain ranges and passes and asked
my father if I had them right: "Are those the Absarokas?" "The
next bridge ought to be the Sweetwater River; tell me when we
get there." He pointed out Big Southern Butte and Twin Buttes,
landmarks of the Snake River Plain, and I tried to find them on
the map.

I made lists, tallying the states I had passed through, the
national parks I had visited. I searched the maps for the little red
squares that marked "Points of Interest"; my questions about

these cued my father's steering-wheel lectures about western history and geology. "Maryhill Museum: what's there, Daddy?" "What happened at Big Hole Battlefield?" "The map shows Crystal Ice Cave ten miles off the highway. Do we have time to go?" From my father, I learned about the Lake Bonneville flood, the differences between gneiss and schist, the route of Lewis and Clark down the Clearwater, and how Chief Tommy Thompson used to fish for salmon at Celilo Falls on the Columbia River before the dams.

My father, Don Trimble, worked as a field geologist for the U.S. Geological Survey for more than thirty years. Every summer, our family left home in Denver to spend the three months between school terms in a town near his field assignment, renting a house near whatever quadrangle he was mapping. In my infancy and early childhood, his mapping projects circled Portland, Oregon. In summers from second grade through high school, we lived in southeastern Idaho, in Aberdeen and in Pocatello.

Setting out across the western states, my mother drove our Dodge, my father the government Jeep. When I rode with my mother, we looked for music on the AM radio, hoping for jazz. When I rode with my father, he told me stories. When we all rode together during vacations, we alternated between these diversions. Boxes of gear for the summer's field season filled the rear of the Jeep and the trunk of the car: dishes, clothes, cameras, map cases, a Brunton compass, rock sample sacks sewn from white canvas and permanently scented with acrid basin and range alkali dust, my bicycle (and, once, in the rear window, my pet-store turtle in a Skippy peanut-butter jar, forgotten and inadvertently boiled when we stopped for lunch one day).

Connection to the natural world can begin with snakes, shells, or stars, birds, beetles, or blackberries. For me, connection started with the land itself, the bones and ligaments of the naked Earth exposed on the rocky surface of the arid West. Geography seeped into me, a bedrock awareness of landscape and place. I learned to pay attention to the flow of scenes framed by the car window. The relatively slow pace and the familiar earthbound perspective of driving made that progression of landscapes comprehensible in a way that today's commonplace airplane travel prohibits.

And I kept staring at the maps. The arbitrarily legislated shapes of national parks printed on them defined the places visually before I ever saw their vistas and wildlife. Today, I close my eyes and conjure these shapes, connected by the meandering red and blue lines of pre-interstate highways, and I can feel the sweaty folds of paper in one hand, the hot rush of air beating and lifting against the other, stretched outward through the open window of the old Dodge.

My childhood in the West—where geology overwhelms biology, lightly vegetated landscape commands attention, and weather is intense—surely gave me an edge in mental map-making. Research suggests that we have map-making genes strung along our DNA, promoting our ability to integrate and organize our experiences of geographic space. Such mental map-making skills clearly gave our hunter-gatherer ancestors an evolutionary advantage.

In researching human development of such cognitive maps, a University of Pittsburgh team of psychologists emphasizes that children and adults begin their descriptions of environments with landmarks. Recognizing landmarks comes, on average, with the full development of the brain, after about four years of age.

Route-finding, remembering a sequence of landmark relationships, comes later. Experience with my own children belies this
model: at one and a half, my son chanted, "Mama, mama," as
soon as we came within five blocks of home on our return from
the babysitter at the end of the day. At two, his sister delightedly
spotted her personal landmarks on our drives around town:
"There's Kevin's office [our pediatrician]. That's Mom's old
work. There's Bartie's house."

Many studies indicate that accurate mental map-making
increases with active participation—with walking through an
environment. Tying together a sequence of places works even
better if those sites are connected by stories. One's own stories
surely work best—the ones we create while walking to school or
exploring a neighborhood gully. Even preschoolers can learn
such sequences—following a baby elephant through a model
jungle, for instance, if they learn the elephant's route in association with a story. Only older children can construct maps in
which routes and smaller regions fit within some larger frame of
reference. Recognizing printed maps as representations of places
can happen as early as three years of age, though grasping their
complexities proceeds slowly after that, in parallel with developing symbolic and spatial skills (just as Piaget, the dominant theo-
rist of child development, would predict).

My own childhood mental maps of the West were fuzzy except
when I could connect them to the stories I knew: the unfolding
of our journeys from Denver to Pocatello, the paths of Lewis
and Clark or the Oregon Trail traced on the maps, geological
"creation legends" absorbed from my father. We learn our homeland from stories, just as we learn nearly everything from stories.
Anthropologist Keith Basso has noted that Apache children in
the Southwest constantly hear their elders link landscape features
with the ethics of living correctly as an Apache. Listen to Benson
Lewis, a Cibecue Apache elder:

I think of that mountain called "white rocks lie above in a compact cluster" as if it were my maternal grandmother. I recall stories of how it once was at that mountain. The stories told to me were like arrows. Elsewhere, hearing that mountain's name, I see it. Its name is like a picture. Stories go to work on you like arrows. Stories make you live right. Stories make you replace yourself.

Each summer evening, my father came home, picked the wood ticks from his clothes, and showered off the dust and reek of sagebrush. After dinner, hunched over the kitchen table, he painstakingly inked his penciled field notes about contacts, dips, and faults onto more permanent mylar maps. In winter, in his Denver office, he worked with the maps still more, writing about the geologic history he had untangled from the land he had walked over. Like most children, what mattered to my father mattered to me. Children notice everything, and with my father as guide, I noticed the land. Once noticed, incoming sensory details needed organizing; they needed names. I grew up valuing the names of landforms, paying attention to where I was in the continent, believing in maps as Scripture.

The first six years of life work their subtle power on us through-out our lives. We remember few specifics. But our bedrock emotional security—our trust—comes from this time. We spend our first years striving to develop what psychologists call "a sense of competence." This drive for mastery—of grasping, crawling, walking, talking, and play—leads to astonishingly rapid and broad learning.

Recent research has surprised us with how emphatically our behavior and personalities are hard-wired by genetics. We start with our general emotional outlook on the world fixed by the magical code of our genes. The bent of personality that makes a girl or boy receptive to natural history may well be something we cannot instill, but rather something with which an individual starts. Nevertheless, genes work in context. No personality or process is independent of environmental and social dimensions.

Seeing with a naturalist's eye is neither eccentric nor artificial. Human brains evolved in the natural world, not in a clinic or lab. Infants prefer patterns a little different, but not *too* different, from those they have seen before. And so, once children learn "bird," they may naturally move on to observing the differences between a robin, a sparrow, a blackbird, and a jay. Infants push out toward the adventure of the unknown, but only so far: the security of the known tempers their reach. This tension between the old and the new, safety versus growth, dominates much of infancy and childhood.

Tiny humans begin their journeys in the haven of family—a safe place, we hope. They test their wills against the giants, the grown-ups, as they struggle to define unique relationships to the world. Each moves from there into the land, adventuring. The expanse of sky and ocean and prairie humble and overwhelm. Nowhere, it seems, do human concerns matter less. And yet, nowhere else is the simple fact of our existence so exhilaratingly clear. Nowhere do so few trivializing and demeaning assaults on egos exist. Nowhere do humans matter more.

By forging connections with plants, animals, and land, by finding ways to experience some relationship to the Earth, individuals can gain a sense of worth. Herein lies security. Edith Cobb, in analyzing the roots of creativity in great thinkers, found that many had experienced a pivotal childhood "discontinuity, an awareness of [one's] own unique separateness and identity, and also a continuity, a renewal of relationship with nature." Cobb marveled at what can grow from this paradox: ". . . a delighted awareness that knowing and being are in some way coincident and continuous . . . and that this kind of knowing is in itself an achievement of psychological balance."

The natural world does not judge. It exists. One route to self-esteem, particularly for shy or undervalued children, lies in the out-of-doors. If, as psychologist Jean Baker Miller asserts, the model of seeking identity by "developing all of one's self in increasingly complex ways, in increasingly complex relation-ships," is desirable, nature is a wonderful place to seek. The sun, the wind, the frogs, and the trees can reassure and strengthen and energize.

The diversity of creatures astonishes us. Cone-nosed kissing bugs and star-nosed moles. Narwhals, sharks, fireflies, and bats. Pythons, tortoises, sequoias. Venus flytraps and black rhinos. Paramecia, amanita; saguaro, tupelo. The endless forms gener ated by evolution subconsciously reassure us of our own validity. No matter that we differ a bit from our peers: difference is the norm. Understanding difference empowers us to grow and to care. The variety of organisms helps to teach tolerance.

The Earth enfolds people in storm or warm sun, in the glory of light filtering through the canopy of deep woods, or in the eddying flow of rivers—without regard for whether we say the right words, wear the right clothes, or believe the right dogma. We are simply human beings setting out into the sanctuary of fields, woods, desert. We have to pay attention, certainly, or we will find ourselves in danger; nonetheless, the land releases us from competition. Such acceptance restores us for the social fight.

"Mine, mine!" resounds through the halls of preschool. In growing toward autonomy, children assert their control through possession. The thrill of *discovering* objects adds uniqueness and intimacy to the act. One friend's son collected "dinosaur eggs" all over the West—an increasingly heavy crate of stream cobbles and river gravel. Rocks, bugs, feathers, bones—many of us remember our treasures.

The summer I was eight, I caught frogs. We were in Aberdeen that field season, a tiny town on the western shore of American Falls Reservoir, surrounded by Idaho potato fields strewn with sprinkler pipe and, beyond, the black lava of the Snake River Plain. What mattered to me, however, was the grid of ditches that lined every street and allowed the mostly Mennonite and Mormon families of the town to flood-irrigate their lawns on hot summer mornings. With two buddies, Tony and Billy, the sons of my father's field partner, I searched for frogs.

The frogs were tiny—young leopard frogs. Adult frogs must have lived nearby, but I remember only the delicate animals an inch long. I lay on the banks and peered under the plank bridges where footpaths crossed the ditches. The silver surface of the water mirrored the hazy cloudless summer sky. With luck, a small amphibious head would break the surface, two bulbous eyes peering off to the sides. I lay in wait, then lunged. I harassed far more individuals than I caught, but the captures excited me as much as the first kill must for a boy in a hunting culture. I plunked the little frogs into empty coffee cans to take them home for a night, and then returned them in the mornings, sluggish but surviving.

Simply discovering that the frogs lived in those ditches in our front yards brought the wildness of other beings into my life. I acted with a child's need to handle and possess them. Each frog was distinct, but I had yet to develop any curiosity about the contrasts among groups of frogs, the species and genera and taxonomic identities of the forms of life that writer Henry Beston called "other nations."

Specificity floated into my consciousness one fall midway through elementary school in the form of golden leaves drifting out of the blue Colorado sky to land on the ground surrounding the church a few doors from our house. We lived in west Denver, where suburbs began their climb to the foothills of the Front Range. Our house lay on the plains, with an old farmhouse across the street, a horse pasture behind us, and undeveloped lots scattered through the neighborhood. The Baptist church buildings stood alone on an otherwise empty block. This was hardly pristine short-grass prairie, but native cottonwoods still dropped clouds of cottony seeds on the spring winds and the signature bird of the Great Plains, magpies, flapped from tree to tree.

I went out to collect leaves for a school project, ironing them between two sheets of wax paper and enlisting my mother to type labels for me. I remember the thrill of appropriating the object, the first step, and then, at the next level, of harvesting the power of its name. This was a new kind of knowledge: cottonwood, catalpa, silver maple, boxelder, locust, elm. These sources of power lay around unclaimed and unowned, there for the taking.

Native peoples who still depend on the land for sustenance acquire such power earlier. Their lives depend on attending to the behavior of their prey animals and on their knowledge of medicinal and food plants. This leads to power in an elemental way—an *appreciation* of the power of other lives.

In developing what the philosopher and ecologist Aldo Leopold called the "land ethic," regard for the wilderness often comes last. First comes a child's involvement with vacant lots, ditch creatures, and the leaves of "weed trees"—discovering what environmental psychologists Rachel and Stephen Kaplan call "nearby nature." Such comparatively mundane experiences lay the foundation for what can develop into Edith Cobb's ideal, "a living ecological relationship between . . . a person and a place"—topophilia, rootedness, placeness, knowing where home is.

Found objects from nature can define a home and nurture self-esteem. Think back to your feelings as a child: wandering, you find wonders, identify them (sometimes), take them home to your room, show them off to friends, and protect them. No one has a conch shell or chip of obsidian or fragile wisp of snakeskin or sack of chestnuts or nub of deer antler just like yours. Your possession is unique; thus, you are unique. Annie Dillard writes eloquently of such experiences in *An American Childhood*. Here is her description of a 1919 dime she once discovered in her alley:

> *Treasure was something you found in the alley. Treasure was something you dug up out of the dirt in a chaotic, half-forbidden, forsaken place far removed from the ordinary comings and goings of people who earned salaries in the light: under some rickety back stairs, near a falling-down pile of discarded lumber, with people yelling at you to get away from there.*
>
> *. . . In spring I pried flat rocks from the damp streambed and captured red and black salamanders. . . . In the fall I walked to collect buckeyes from lawns. Buckeyes were wealth.*

The key then is to plant the buckeye, feed the salamander, invent a story about the dime. With these acts of extension, children begin to cultivate relationship—and the concomitant risks and rewards of sharing, of giving, of love. By moving beyond simple ownership they avoid the trap of permanently linking their self-esteem with what is only the first step—acquisition. Eventually, the discovery suffices for power; observation serves as possession; and we leave these objects where we find them, transcending the old dead-end of human domination over nature.

Experiencing this adventure firsthand is crucial. Piaget himself said, "In order for a child to understand something he must construct it for himself, he must reinvent it . . . if in the future individuals are to be formed who are capable of creativity and not simply repetition." British planner Robin Moore, in his fine study of children's use of neighborhood spaces, *Childhood's Domain*, speaks of the powerful "qualities of openness, diversity, manipulation, explorability, anonymity, and wildness" offered by what he calls "rough ground" in the midst of urban and suburban communities:

> *The indeterminancy of rough ground allows it to become a play-partner, like other forms of creative partnership: actress-audience, potter-clay, photographer-subject, painter-canvas. The exploring/creating child is not making "art" so much as using the landscape as a medium for understanding the world by continually destructing/reconstructing it. Where is this vital activity to be carried on if every part of the child's environment is spoken for to meet the economic, social and cultural needs of the adult community?*

Several surveys reveal where children make their contacts with the natural world; they often name the same key ingredients: small places, trees, and water (brooks and frog ponds). As Gary Nabhan noted in the previous chapter, children favor small places close by—with dirt, trees, bushes, and "loose parts"—to build and dabble in (at their best, within a hundred yards of their homes). Trees, as writer Colin Ward describes them in the British countryside, "can be climbed and hidden behind; they can become forts or bases; with their surrounding vegetation and roots, they become dens and little houses; they provide shelter, landmarks and privacy; fallen, they become part of an obstacle course or material for den-building; near them you find birds, little animals, conkers [chestnuts], fallen leaves, mud, fir cones and winged seeds; they provide a suitable backdrop for every conceivable game of the imagination."

Middle childhood comes after what psychologists call the five-to-seven shift. The brain is finally fully developed. Children become capable of far more sophisticated learning, what Piaget calls "concrete operations." In other primates, this shift leads right into puberty. Humans, however, have postponed the hormonal rush until the teenage years, opening up a six-year interval when childhood brains receive and learn in a uniquely fresh, receptive, and playful way. Edith Cobb emphasizes the potency of this time when children are "in love with the universe" and poised "halfway between inner and outer worlds." Here, she says, lie "latent power and purpose, the seeds of the writer's art, the painter's vision, the explorer's passion." As Melvin Konner notes in his fine book, *Childhood*: "These are the years when the child is seen by societies throughout the world as a vessel into which knowledge, skill, and tradition—in short, culture—can be steadily and reliably poured."

Writer and educator Paul Shepard speaks of "the ark of the mind," a lovely phrase. "A decade, from the beginnings of speech to the onset of puberty, is all we have to load the ark." With animals, with plants, with place, with sunrises and moonsets. With wildness.

This is the decade that I have remembered in my stories of maps and frogs, the years in which I was a vessel for my teachers, family, and peers to fill. I vividly remember the last travels of those years, park by national park, snapshot by snapshot. The year I turned thirteen, my ability to focus on the same experiences disappeared for a time beneath a haze of hormonal pyrotechnics.

Adolescents take whatever we have given them, and run. On this mad dash, they seem to close their eyes and run in unpredictable directions. As parents, we try to keep them from running off cliffs. We hope they will climb mountains and not be trapped in one or another disastrous morass. But our control is disappearing fast. Our children are off on their own journeys, carrying with them whatever we have given them, knowingly or unknowingly.

Adolescence for me was too early to feel a part of the naturalist and philosopher Joseph Wood Krutch's "great chain of life," to understand the land in context, with an awareness of interdependencies. I neither knew enough nor had sufficient experience. Adulthood legally begins at eighteen or twenty-one for good reason.

I turned twenty-one and entered adulthood in several of the usual ways in 1971. And I returned once more to learning the names of trees.

For a college field project in an introductory botany class, I censused conifers along a thousand vertical feet of switchbacking trail on St. Charles Peak in Colorado's Wet Mountains. I learned to identify six evergreens in addition to the deciduous aspen I already knew, and analyzed their elevational distributions and limits. Never before had I noticed the specificity of trees in their environment. Now, I did. Douglas fir. Engelmann spruce. Common juniper. White fir. Subalpine fir. Limber pine. Seedling, sapling, adult.

In retrospect, knowing where an awareness of trees has led me, I see the discovery of their lives as just as pivotal as any other landmark of maturing. For the first time, I passed into what biologist E. O. Wilson calls "the naturalist's trance," when my connections to other creatures mattered as much as my humanity. I saw details with a little of the attentiveness of a writer. My ability to see and understand beyond my personal boundaries passed a crucial threshold.

Ever since, I have seen these trees as my friends. When they grow along my path, I reach out to them, draw their needles through my hands, and smile. I say their names, an acknowledgment of kinship—like a formal genealogy, another chapter of Scripture. *Pseudotsuga. Picea. Juniperus. Abies concolor. Pinus flexilis.*

"*Pseudotsuga.* Douglas fir. I am here, too."

Not every child has the predilection to become a naturalist. And it may take time to develop. For instance, I did not see beyond my adolescent self until twenty-one.

I started lucky—with a secure middle-class background, decent self-esteem, curiosity, and a privileged education. My childhood experiences with maps and geography and exposure to open country gave me an underlying understanding of environment ready to populate with animals and plants. Not until chance encounters in my last years of college, however—my best friend's passion for field biology, another friend's stories of working as a park ranger, encountering mentors—did I begin to *see* as a naturalist, watching the telephone poles for raptors, carrying binoculars to identify the warblers in riparian woods, learning the telltale characters of borage, mustard, and sedge. Only then did I come to believe that natural history was as important as civil rights, American literature, or having a romance in one's life. And not until I began to read the literature of natural history could I articulate my belief in the Earth as grounding and faith and guide.

None of us can predict or control the career or avocational choices of our children. All we can do is introduce, try to prevent prejudice, battle gender stereotypes, teach by the example of our own attention and wonder. All we can do is recite from the Scripture of maps and field guides. Give names to the mountains and rivers, give names to the trees. Give voice to the emotions that storms and tundra flowers, young bison and soaring ravens can pull from us.

As parents, we can take our children with us to the land. We can be there with them as they climb on rocks, play in streams and waves, dig in the rich soil of woods and gardens, putter and learn. Here, on the land, we learn from each other. Here, our children's journey begins.

S.T.

Going Truant: The Initiation
of Young Naturalists

It must have been late spring, for I remember that the ice had already broken and the cold weather had passed from the Lake Michigan shoreline. I was a high school dropout, an unruly dissident not quite drinking or voting age; in short, a rebel without any good cause. I was gandy dancing on a track repair crew in the steel mills—doing anything I could to keep from working indoors—and hoping to save enough money to try my luck again with formal education in the fall.

At that moment, my mind was neither on the work before me nor on the prospects of school. I had glanced up from driving spikes into railroad ties, and had caught sight of a half-dozen blue herons loping by above me, looking for a place to land.

Half my life has passed since that sighting, but to this day those herons loom as large in my mind's eye as if they were Jurassic pterodactyls. I can still see them flying low in the heavy, pollution-laden air above the steel mills of Gary, Indiana: their deep wing beats, their hoarse squawks as they called to one another over the mechanical cacophony of foundries, refineries, and finishing plants.

At first, I thought the herons were simply passing by the mills and train depots as quickly as they could, for how would they see the blast furnaces, pig iron piles, and cinder-covered railroad yards as anything more than horrors to migrate over, to escape? But I saw them circle, as if searching for some former habitats of sandy swales and marshes. Few such habitats had persisted after industry arrived in the area, and the Lake Michigan shoreline could no longer be followed eastward out of Chicago, since dredgings and land fills had forever altered the shore's natural configuration. And yet, these birds appeared to be following a much older mental map. They may have been pulled to this place by genetically encoded memory, as if it were aligned with some magnetic pole along their ancient migration route. Perhaps the interdunal lagoons here had sheltered the rookeries of their ancestors since the time of the last minor Ice Age advance several thousand years ago.

The herons inspected the slag heap nearest to me, where a shallow pond had once lain between two ridges of sand. They slowly flew to the next debris-filled depression, then the next, then the next, until they passed out of my sight, and beyond the manufacture of steel, chemicals, and car parts, on toward the tenuous refuge of the newly decreed Indiana Dunes National Lakeshore. I stood there for another moment, imagining their trail toward other primordial pitstops, following the path of their predecessors for millennia.

It was then that I had my own magnetic encounter with an encoded legacy—a continuity with former generations of my own kind—that had buried deep within my own consciousness. I realized that no matter where I was, I had the capacity to see the world as freshly as any naturalist could. Even in the most damaged of habitats, in the drudgery of the most menial labor, whatever wildlife remained could still pull at me deeply enough to disrupt business-as-usual. The behavior of these birds had overtaken my imagination, even though I had never demonstrated any scholarly inclinations toward ornithology. The herons awakened capabilities in me that formal education had not yet cultivated, for I felt welling up within me a profound desire to know those birds better. I felt the weight of the spike mall in my hand

and the burden of the labor I had before me, yet my heart flew with the herons.

This brief experience became for me a benchmark. From then on, I began to gather the skills, and even some of the accoutrements, of a bonafide naturalist. At the time, I thought I might be embarking on a new career that would allow me to leave those factories and rails far behind me. I did not realize until later that it was not a *new* career; the vocation of being a naturalist on one's home ground is truly the oldest profession in the world. Several million years of foraging and hunting by our hominid ancestors had hard-wired into me—into all of us through natural selection—the capacity to see the world as a naturalist. I was preadapted to give my full attention to those herons.

The heron incident was not the first time that birds had riveted my attention; probably each of us has retained some image of animals that goes back as far as our memory goes. My mother still kids me about our earliest verbal battle, when I was not much older than three or four. I was sitting in the sand, playing at the edge of our backyard, where a small dune spilled into a small wetland. She called from the porch for me to come to the house and eat; I replied that I wanted to stay outdoors a little while longer. She repeated her request; I remained defiant. Finally, she ordered, "Gary Paul, get into the house right now, or I'll give you a spanking!"

I broke into tears and howls, then stood up to brush the sand off of my corduroy overalls. Just then, a bluejay flew over me, cawing raucously, apparently responding to my own outburst. "See!" I whimpered, pointing out the bluejay to my mother. "He's mad at you too! Even the bluejays want me to stay outside!"

From my first day of kindergarten to my first day of graduate studies in botany twenty years later, school was synonymous with staying indoors, out of touch with the most elemental aspects of life. Within my initial hour of formal education, I was yanked up by the shoulders and scolded for crawling behind a piano to curl up to sleep in a bookshelf. I had quickly come to the conclusion that Mrs. Wiltrout, the kindergarten teacher, was going to bore us simply by *talking* all morning long, so I thought I'd rest up for when she let us out for recess just before lunch.

I had similar difficulty with the first day of graduate courses in botany two decades later. After a full summer of learning about desert plants from Indian people, I fell asleep in the front row of an air-conditioned lecture hall while being told that the Linnaean system was *the* only way to classify and study plants. I was simply better adapted to learning by doing, outdoors, than to learning by abstract formula.

And yet, from Mrs. Wiltrout's first insistence on order in the classroom, to my uncompleted junior year before I left high school for good, I can recall only three school-sponsored field trips for nature study. We were allowed gym class and playground recess, of course, but little time beyond the manicured confines of the schoolyard. During my first twelve years of school, I figure that my teachers offered a total of less than six uninterrupted hours in the marvelous natural laboratory at our doorstep: the Indiana Dunes, a hodgepodge of buried forests, quaking bogs, and mountains of sand. Even in a place so well-suited for nature study, my teachers kept us inside classrooms for a thousand hours for every one hour they took us into the field. In urban centers with no easy access to natural areas, I'm sure my contemporaries suffered even more severe sentences.

Throughout those years, only one teacher took my class on an overnight into "the woods," where, in a winterized cabin, we were lectured on Thoreau's experiences at Walden while drinking hot cocoa and eating *s'mores*. A single science instructor encouraged us to learn—on our own time—the names and traits of the many shorebirds and waterfowl that frequented the habitats within a mile of the school. All the rest of my formal environmental education before college was channeled through dissecting scopes, books, films, and ready-made flip charts. The messages were clear. Nature should be treated as a distant abstraction. Biology is one of many exercises in *logos*, reasoning, but has very little to do with *bios*, life. Our teachers prepared us for careers to be spent within buildings. Whatever one could possibly learn outdoors hardly mattered in the "real world."

It should come as no surprise that I learned more about the natural world while playing hookey than I ever learned in the classroom. Perhaps that is as it should be, for as writer Franklin Burroughs has quipped, "Nature education is a contradiction of terms, because formal education is where you're *supposed to be*, and nature is where you go when you're *truant*."

In my case, I ditched afternoon classes whenever the hordes of migratory waterfowl appeared in Long's Lake, less than two miles from school. I would watch clouds of geese descend onto the water, so thickly crowded they had to clamber over each other to find a patch of water large enough for their tails. I ventured onto ice floes nudging the Lake Michigan shoreline, never falling more than waist deep through the ice, and never figuring out why short eared owls spent so much time on floes far from where rodents might congregate. In early fall, I body-surfed as the waves rose up before a large storm, holding out as long as I could against the increasing undertow, and before the lightning shows came too close for comfort. Friends camped with me in remnant stands of jack pine, on old dunes where other conifers had been logged out after the great Chicago fire. Those tough, wayward trees became symbols for me, for they were true survivors of all sorts of adversities, natural as well as man-made.

I have always assumed that such moments of wonder with the natural world have been experienced by most, if not all, people. And yet, when I read polls that claim that only 8 percent of American adults feel that the quality of environment is a major issue in their lives, while over 90 percent of our children feel it is *the* major issue which concerns them, I am amazed at how few adults follow their earlier inclinations to be fully involved with the natural world. Even when our society concedes that fuzzy animals and pretty plants can be engaging for children, it does not grant that that anyone should waste his or her time on such things after the age of puberty. As Swedish botanist Peter Kalm complained of adult Americans in 1750, most take "little account of Natural History . . . that science being . . . looked upon as a mere trifle, and the pastime of fools." Western civilization has encouraged its leisure class to indulge in very few recreational pursuits that extend beyond gyms, pools, ball courts, and raceways. Our society's token nature-lovers are treated as overgrown but harmless juveniles, dillydallying away their time and money on matters undeserving of serious attention by mature adults. And that is where our society might be wrong, dead wrong.

Earlier in our history as a species, nearly all individuals went through rites of passage in the wilderness. These rites transformed children into adults—adults who could hardly forget the importance of nature-as-teacher for the rest of their lives. Western society today fails to provide such rites of passage to a significant portion of our population. As Paul Shepard has suggested in *Nature and Madness*, those who as adolescents fail to pass through such rites remain in an arrested state of immaturity. They lack the tangible experience and symbolic touchstones that would otherwise enable them to become mentally and emotionally whole, and potentially at peace with the outer world. Instead, they feel that all the problems are "out there," so they try to make the world over in their own image, or blame others for their plight.

Worse yet, the disaffection found in much of today's street graffiti, videos, and rap music indicate that schools are now offering youth even less experience which they consider to be of lasting value. The physical and social survival skills adolescents so urgently need are not being offered to them through conventional education. It is not surprising that over 28 percent of those who currently enter American high schools will not complete their coursework over the next four years, and even those who do may be chronically distracted by the guns, drugs, and alcohol that they take with them into the classroom. Most will be forced to learn what they have to learn about survival from sources entirely beyond the schoolyard, with little guidance from adults.

Fortunately for some youth, there are a few programs scattered across the country dedicated to the difficult, often painful task of working with high school dropouts. Programs such as Vision-Quest, a Tucson-based effort, have helped thousands of troubled teenagers gain the discipline required to complete their schooling or other kinds of training programs in their chosen fields.

Bob Burton, who in 1972 helped to found Vision-Quest, has told me that the continuing need for a rite of passage for teenagers became clear to him while he was working with Crow, Shoshone, and Paiute teens in the late 1960s. "It was while I was trying to deal with delinquent Indian kids on reservations in the Great Basin and Northern Plains. I began to learn what older cultures here in North America had done to give kids a sense of who they were, by getting them away from everything . . ."

Over the years, Burton has helped to refine Vision-Quest's programs so that they are not directed simply at removing troubled teenagers from the material trappings of urban life—including drugs, alcohol, and electronic fantasies—so readily accessible in cities. Vision-Quest places these youth in situations that demand considerable growth, emotionally, socially, and physically.

"Our program now provides kids with eight to ten months of wilderness encounter, of serious physical challenges. And they are carefully guided so that they learn some real survival skills from our staff. Again, it's like the traditional vision-quests: the elders would help them build on what they learned from the experience, by interpreting it in a larger context. Most of these kids are from fragmented families and haven't felt too secure in the world. They need to feel centered, as Native Americans historically felt when they stood on the four cardinal directions in a medicine wheel, with the continuing presence of Father Sky and Mother Earth. . . . We want to give our kids something similar, a consistent way to be at peace with themselves and secure in this world."

I was curious about the kinds of physical challenges that best engage the Vision-Quest participants.

"The kids," Burton told me, "have to be responsible for getting mules, mustangs, dogs, and camels fed, and moving with the wagon train first thing in the morning. Sometimes they must move seventeen miles in the morning before beginning their coursework for the day. We have also had good success with teepee camps, and sailing excursions in the Sea of Cortez."

He continued. "The typical kid in our programs left high school two or three years before, unable to spend all day long manipulating symbols in a classroom. These kids learned real early on to be quitters. But in nature, you can't quit. You're faced with real physical challenges. The kid who can't learn to face such challenges from us may look for them in sports, or he may spin off to look for them in gang warfare on the streets. That's the wrong place. We try to give kids the kind of challenges that will get them ready for more school . . . "

Burton clearly sees his program as giving troubled kids a second start. If he can break their cycle of failure, anger, and lowered self-esteem, the kids who develop new competencies can then transfer to other education programs without additional failures being inevitable. But to keep the vicious cycle from returning, they need to see that problems at home can be resolved as well. Many of them have grown up facing daily conditions far more desperate than having to take down a teepee in a storm, or provide sufficient feed and water for a mule on a hundred-degree day.

"It's a barren, impoverished desert out there for them right now," Burton said. "It's a place that needs to be planted with the appropriate seeds . . ."

While Vision-Quest has served over ten thousand teenagers during its twenty years of existence, it is not the only nor the most widely heralded program initiating young people into adulthood. In 1974, Canadian educator Maurice Gibbons proposed that the "walkabout" rite of passage of Australian aborigines could serve as a model for North American students who were searching for "the right passage from childhood and school." His article in the *Phi Delta Kappan* inspired a variety of programs that led students out of their schools into both their communities and their natural surroundings. From the Humanities Walkabout at Broad Ripple High in Indianapolis, to the Challenge Education project for student-teachers at the University of Wyoming in Cheyenne, these efforts have been ranked among the top experiential education programs in the United States during the last decade.

Most of these programs have several features in common. First, participants must demonstrate their courage, endurance, and practical skill in facing the challenges of an unfamiliar social or physical environment. Next, the students must devise independent, practical studies outside the school setting that draw upon their capacities for reasoning and creative expression. Finally, they must accomplish some volunteer service on behalf of their community, taking responsibility for carrying a work project to its completion. At the end of their Walkabout experiences, the participants cite their accomplishments before a gathering of adults from their community, to show their readiness to become full-fledged members of that community. A celebration usually follows.

Some educators complain that after a number of years, Walkabout programs in high schools can become too "prepackaged" and formula-oriented. This criticism has motivated others to adapt the basic concept of Walkabout to address the concerns of each new wave of students and adjust to the opportunities peculiar to their communities.

To me, it seems that the key is in not diluting the essential power of the archetypal rite of passage by letting the experience drift too far away from the connecting ground of nature. A project which simply allows a student to interview merchants in an urban industrial center offers little more than business as usual. It will not have the same feeling of elemental challenge and passage as, for example, a raft trip down the Ohio River during the spring flood, inspired by *Huckleberry Finn*.

Perhaps the simplest, most stripped-down rites are ultimately the most powerful. I once worked with inner-city minority children from Chicago in a program called "Human Beginnings," which included an entire week on birthing, puberty, marriage, and death rites. One of the instructors was a young man named Bakyoko Bakassa, who grew up near Abidjan in the Ivory Coast. His entire body trembled when he told of his own people's rites:

"I cannot tell you how we do the entire thing, for our initiations are so complicated, involve so many things! The boys of a certain age are taken out far from the village with a master, into the forest to a mud-walled shelter with a conical straw roof, to live a couple of weeks together."

"You see, this Human Beginnings program, what you learn here. . . . I am interested in it because you learn the secrets of life, of the world, of the tribe; you eat together, you cook special things; you take time away from the routine life in the village."

He laughed quietly. "The master, he taught in a circle like this. And he put the boys through various ordeals; many got scared. It was hard on them. But every boy, when he came back to the village, you could notice something *changed* in his countenance. They seemed so different afterwards."

"How different are these dudes?" A young black girl from south Chicago asked him.

"See, one goes from being a boy to being a man. Now, he is responsible. Before, he was not. He can get married after that, after the master initiates him, after he has had the circumcision. We say, 'He can take his own boat on the river now.'"

"Did you go through it that way?" One of the teenaged boys asked, a little horrified by what he read between the lines in Baky's account.

Baky responded with a twinkle in his eye. "I tried not to go through the initiation when my time came. Older boys had given me the story of what had gone on with them, and imagining such terrible things made me run away when it came to be my time." He then told how he had gone away from his village to get a formal education, and how, when he had returned, he had expected everyone to respect him for his accomplishments. That did not occur. Some of his contemporaries would not talk to him. The older men still treated him like a little boy.

"Finally, the village elders said that I had to make up for not going through my initiation at the right time. When I turned eighteen, they gave me another chance: to become a man in the eyes of the people, I had to fight one of the strongest men in the village. So I agreed. . . . We took all of our clothes off," he said, with a sweep of his arm across his carefully-tailored French clothing, "keeping nothing on but our loincloths. You know?"

Baky began to laugh, amused by the memory. "I wrestled this man *for three straight days*! Everyone in the village took sides, his or mine. They remain split over the outcome to this day. That was five years ago, and the man was big, far bigger than me, and I did not know how to bring him down at the time. Since then, I have received my black belt in karate." His hand slashed the air, and he offered a quick kick toward a tree. "So that this fall, when I return, I am confident that I shall finally beat him!"

The kids were overwhelmed by the thought of Baky having to go back and face his foe five years later. "Is it worth it?" one asked.

"Yes, for the secrets of the village, and of my tribe, the Malinke, are told with these initiations." He cleared his throat and then said emphatically, "It is also that initiation is a second birth. Yes. The Gikuyu people of Kenya, in fact, begin their rite this way: the child to be initiated crouches, curled underneath his mother's body, for she stands tall above him. A rope is tied from her hips to his waist, representing the umbilical cord. The mother then wails, crying painfully, as if she is going through labor for him again. After several hours of this, the rope is cut, *like that*!" Baky's hand swiftly cut the air in front of us, leaving us gasping.

"From there," he said quietly, "the boy is turned out, to become a man."

———

For a boy to become a man in such a way, and for a girl to become a woman in her own way, is to fulfill a quintessential human drama. For some two million years, we have had the capacity for language, storytelling, and ritual theater, launched by our older capacity for gesture and elaborated by our peculiar ability to use symbols for guiding us on our way through this world. During much of our history, animals have been among the key symbols we have used to sort out options for ourselves. Each kind of animal has its own adaptive strategy, a distinctive way of dealing with the dilemmas posed by this world. And so when young men and women choose totem animals—which they are often charged to do at the time of their initiation rite—they settle upon ones that embody particular behaviors with which they personally identify. The swift-running woman may select the gazelle; the hard-hitting hunter may choose the puma. These totem animals suggest ways to survive, to thrive, to lead rich lives.

Such animals are metaphorical guides, but for the metaphors to work we first have to know the animals themselves; not only their names, but their appearances, their behaviors, and their movements as well. If linguists are correct, much of earliest use of language was devoted to naming animals. After they became recognized and named, we could coherently link our observations regarding their activities over time.

And so, very early on in human evolution, we became naturalists. Our curiosity about other species may not be uniquely human, but it is much more pronounced in *Homo sapiens* than it is in other surviving primates. As Dorothy Cheney and Robert Seyfarth have observed, for example,

> *Vervet monkeys are poor naturalists. They seem disinclined to collect information about their environment when that information is not directly relevant to their own survival. Vervets do not seem to know*

that hippos stay in the water during the daytime or that particular shorebirds do not occur in dry woodlands. These data are perhaps not surprising, but they do point out a potential difference between monkeys and human beings, who are naturally curious about much of their environment and who engage in many activities that have little practical value to survival.

Our evolutionary history has clearly suited us to a peculiar kind of nature-sensing, relative to that of other primates. We have come to some of our senses in subtropical savannas, while others evolved while we were still hangers-on in the trees of tropical rainforests. In any case, the skills which we use to study field biology today—and to accomplish many other tasks— emerged early on in human evolution, as we practiced our foraging for wild plants and animals, and sorted out some of these species as potentially viable symbols in our lives. Moreover, anthropologists now contend that our very ability to symbolize and make projections into the future developed as an indirect benefit of our brain's complex adaptations that better accommodated the manipulatory and throwing behaviors involved in hunting, fishing, and foraging for arborescent fruits.

When I was the boy who stood on the tracks, spike mall in hand, twenty years ago, I had just begun to realize that I was a ready-made naturalist. My eyes and hands were already capable of certain complex sorting and identifying tasks—which I have used every time I have assisted some plant taxonomist or zoologist in our field studies—but I did not realize until recently that those skills had been in place since the time hominids first gave up free-swinging in trees for a life on the open ground. Once we relaxed our grip on tree limbs, our hands became free to accomplish the manual maneuvers that other naturalists and I now take for granted: pulling up an armload of grasses, prying open crayfish shells, knocking a fruit off an overhanging branch, measuring the girth of a tree trunk, or tying knots. Our increasingly long, flexible thumbs, opposable to the rest of our fingers, now enable us to hold binoculars, focus them, and see even farther into space. As a young railroad worker in the dunes, I was soon to turn in my spike mall for a pair of field glasses, but was still unaware that hominid evolution had endowed me with the ability to hold either item. My manual dexterity and perceptual abilities were there no matter which I chose.

That day at Lake Michigan, I made a rite of passage, an odd circling-back before I could go forward. I rejected a career as a railroad worker—a job that my fathers and maternal uncles had done with skill and dignity—and turned back to the soil and plants that had sustained my grandfathers and their forebearers in more direct ways. Like my granduncle, Papa John Nabhan, I would become for a time a harvester and vendor of vegetables, a man who traded cross-culturally in the harvests of the green world. Like Papa, I had to be outside if I were to survive.

Sooner or later, though, my pursuits would take me farther and farther away from the cultivated lands where Papa had gleaned the fruits and vegetables to feed his family. Although I ended up obtaining an agricultural degree, lives more wild than those I ever found in cultivated, weeded fields kept calling me. I wanted to go where neither houses nor plants stood in manicured rows. I had a hankering to be out in the unmanaged places where I could use skills much older even than those developed by agriculturists.

I wanted to get to places where the open, savanna-like quality of the dunes and marshlands had not been completely overwhelmed, where herons still nested. I had grown up loving the long vistas that dune promontories offered, and the routine visual exercises required by that landscape had given me chances to identify birds at some distance with considerable precision. Perhaps my predilection for open savanna was set in genetic memory, and reinforced within my first seven years of living where a few oaks, beach cherries, and cottonwoods had grown up among the dunes grasses—a landscape similar to the African terrain in which humankind was born.

At the same time, I could smell and taste where I was just as easily as I could see it. I had become accustomed to the ambivalent fragrance of the lakeshore: a fresh breeze off the lake mixed with the iron and sulfur oxides of the mills. I often drew upon an olfactory sense which had evolved to alert my species to ripened fruit or tubers ready for digging, and to repulse us from eating rotten meat and toxic leaves. Although I could not easily identify plants and animals only by their smells, I had become accustomed to telling birds apart by their characteristic squawks, cheeps, and caws. Even before humans diverged from other primates, we had gained the capacity to associate other species' warning calls with the possibility of imminent danger, and remember them by onomatopoetic names. I had unconsciously glanced up from my work as soon as I had heard the first set of squawks from the migrating herons.

And so, in the middle of an industrial wasteland, I passed through a window of time, from the modern world, to an ancient, much more enduring one. I had suddenly realized the blessings of certain primordial skills we all have, skills I could use in the fullest possible way if I were to become a naturalist. At that moment, I chose to refine and apply them toward whatever work I would find in the service of the earth.

What I didn't know until later was that I had also begun to walk the path of a man. I did not begin my own path simply by rejecting the livelihood my uncles and fathers had shared; I began too by taking responsibility for searching out an older path, one that had been nearly obliterated by the industrial world—a path analogous to what the herons were tracking along their migration route.

In that moment of choosing between the chaos of the dunes and the linear order of the railroad, I had not the slightest inkling of where that chosen path would lead me. And yet, I had the same unfailing faith as the herons that I was moving in the right direction. Suddenly, I had gained a sure-footedness along a trail where formerly, I had been stumbling. Out of the blue, the herons had blessed my day. They offered my imagination the possibility of finding places where I too would thrive, and thrive in a way that I would never have felt had I stayed among the foundries, the refineries, and the blast furnaces.

G.P.N.

A Land of One's Own

▲   ▲   ▲   ▲   ▲   ▲   ▲   ▲   ▲   ▲

I have been startled by a series of conversations I have had with women over the past several years.

In the mid-1980s, I searched for women to include in a natural history writing anthology I was editing. I found far fewer female than male writers who had generated a body of published work centered on land-based essays. For the book, I selected essays by four women (Annie Dillard, Gretel Ehrlich, Sue Hubbell, and Ann Zwinger) and eleven men. In my introduction, I speculated about why relatively few women today write and publish nature essays, and, in a more recent piece, I addressed the question again. In response, women have suggested answers, offered insights, and illuminated the issues. Much of what they say circles around childhood socialization. Now, I have a daughter and a son. Gender issues matter more to me than ever before. But I have been surprised at how little I understand these issues. I am a naïve man.

During the sixties and early seventies, when the young women who were my friends demanded that I unlearn the gender stereotypes I had absorbed in high school, I was shocked at the thoughtless chauvinism of my values. In the years since, I have blithely assumed that for myself and most other men, unlearning and relearning had been successful, that these were no longer big issues for most of us, that men and women had achieved equality in many fundamental ways. Even if such equality did not yet play out in practicalities like salaries and access to power, surely we were close to such a time.

As I write this, my two children are nearing their second and fifth birthdays. Becoming a parent challenges all of my comfortable presumptions. My children, my wife, and I face a long passage together. We can remain complacent about nothing. How does gender affect each of our relationships with the earth? Will the experience of my daughter inevitably differ from that of my son? Gender issues come up in virtually every topic we write about in this book, but these issues raise more questions than they yield answers.

I do know that my old assumptions are toppling. I have plenty of learning and unlearning left to do. What follows in this essay is an investigation, not a conclusion, conducted by a relatively new father.

Start with nature essayists, who started me off on gender issues more than six years ago.

The bent of personality that makes for a natural history writer comes from a need to write, a love of landscape, insatiable curiosity about the details of life in that landscape, a dedication to accuracy in understanding those details, devotion to language and image rooted in imagination rather than science, and a desire to ponder one's relationship to the earth—qualities that could come together in anyone, but surely are rooted in childhood. This seems a genderless description. But where are the female nature essayists?

From the late eighteenth to the early twentieth century, American women naturalists had to elude dominant male expectations to slip into the field. Of the twenty-five of these pioneers whose lives Marcia Bonta relates in *Women in the Field*, "eleven never married. Five others started careers only after the early deaths of their husbands, two married in middle age after they had done the bulk of their natural history work, six married supportive males in similar fields, and only two were actively discouraged by their mates. All but two of the married women were childless."

Rachel Carson, the archetype of female naturalist writers, described herself as a "rather solitary child." Her mother gave her critical encouragement to find her way, nurturing her reading and exploration of the natural world, almost from infancy. According to her biographer, Paul Brooks, Carson "assumed from early childhood that she was going to be a writer." She sold her first story at eleven, and then went on to formal studies in biology. It took years for Carson to realize that she could be both a writer *and* a scientist: "I thought I had to be one or the other; it never occurred to me, or apparently anyone else, that I could combine the two careers."

Rachel Carson had an additional challenge; though single, she raised two nieces and a grandnephew. Fieldwork, thinking, and writing require a substantial amount of solitude. Solitude takes time, and caregivers to children have no time. Our children demand attention and need care. They ask questions, and parents must answer. The number of decisions that go into a week of parenting astonishes me. Women have known for centuries what I have just discovered: going to work every day is far easier than staying home raising children.

And another paradox: in the few years we live with our children and hope to influence them—to pass on our best values and most thoughtful concerns—we are trying to choose just the right words and tone while much of the time functioning in a state of exhaustion, impatience, and frustration. We are in good shape if we can honestly leave resentment off this list. Thoughtful parenting requires time to think, and parents of young children do not have time to think.

One middle-aged female writing student spoke to me of feeling she lacked the freedom to "play hooky in nature"; it is an act of leisure men indulge in while women stay at home, keeping domestic life in order. Men often can justify poking around in the woods as a part of their profession, or as part of an acceptably manly activity like hunting or fishing. Women, for generations circumscribed by conventional values, must purposefully create opportunities for solitude, for exploration of nature or ideas, for writing.

The dominant culture makes it hard for a woman to say: "I am a writer. Leave me alone for eight hours today. And the next day. And the next." She can more easily find small spaces around the edges of other obligations after the kids are asleep, sitting at the kitchen table or at a bedside desk. Nature-based essays require at least an afternoon escape over the back fence and into the neighborhood park—again, a seemingly straightforward experience not so easy for many women to build into their lives.

Scholar Carolyn Heilbrun identifies the core of the problem in *Writing a Woman's Life*: "Women come to writing . . . simultaneously with self-creation." Writing involves laying claim to space, both physical and psychic. Publishing involves publicly laying claim to power—the power of print. This act of self-expression is daunting for anyone.

For women, the challenge is twofold. Every woman acculturated to docile and stereotypical femininity must reinvent herself, first as a person, then as a writer. Heilbrun notes that women come to this point (if they reach it at all) most often after a passage, an "awakening," and most often after fifty. Men have a "safety net" of other male writers as mentors and models; women work without a net. "How are [women] to imagine forms and language they have never heard? How are they to live to write, and to write that other women may live?" Heilbrun's conclusion: "There will be narratives of female lives only when women no longer live their lives isolated in the houses and stories of men."

Jean Baker Miller, psychiatrist and author of the classic *Toward a New Psychology of Women*, notes that American women are "discouraged from serious testing of themselves." She goes on: "In fact, women are encouraged to believe that if they do go through the mental and emotional struggle of self-development, the end result will be disastrous—they will forfeit the possibility of having any close relationships." And so society tells girls that they had better stay inside; dire consequences will follow if they do not.

Miller makes the case that women are encouraged to believe that, "ideally, all activity should lead to an increased emotional connection with others. . . . Further, when they do pursue their self-interests, women have difficulty in allowing this kind of activity to be a basis for a sense of their self-worth. Women's sense of worth is not supposed to come from this quarter. . . . Indeed, women's sense of self becomes very much organized around being able to make and then to maintain affiliations and relationships."

I have been clueless for years. Cloistered in the isolated world of a writer, married to a professional woman, I have assumed that liberation has worked for most of the women and men I know, that gender no longer was much of an issue. I was wrong, of course. Culture has more staying power than that. My question about the lack of female natural history writers begins to look naïve, as well. Women have unequal access to most professional pursuits; female writers of all kinds face a literary culture that values them less than men.

As Virginia Woolf made clear in her history of "women and

fiction," *A Room of One's Own*, from the sixteenth century on, any aspiring woman writer had to confront the prevailing maxim: "No woman of sense and modesty could write books." Woolf marvels that Jane Austen and her cohorts could write such fine novels with "the influences of the common sitting-room" as their sole literary training and defining experience. Not only could a woman never venture into the fields alone, she could not go anywhere alone.

At the end of *A Room of One's Own*, Woolf states her hopes for the future: if women "have five hundred a year each of us and rooms of our own; if we have the habit of freedom and the courage to write exactly what we think; if we escape a little from the common sitting-room and see human beings not always in their relation to each other but in relation to reality; and the sky, too, and the trees or whatever it may be in themselves," then women will be free to write, free to plunge into experiences with wildness, "to go about the business of life."

As parents who hope to connect our children to nature, we must recognize this cultural bias, and then do our best to overwhelm it. Our daughters, especially, need to know that we believe they can do anything—*especially* those activities traditionally decreed masculine. Poking around outdoors and writing for publication clearly are two such activities.

Cultural barriers and fears keep many of our daughters away from the woods and the fields. Tomboys are acceptable only until they reach the threshold of adolescence. Then, they are told, they must climb down from the trees they love and act "a proper lady." At this point, young women begin to live within a paradox. They are taught to spend their time attracting men, but they also are taught to fear violence from men. As a result, women may crave solitude but many fear being alone in the land-scape. Over and over, they tell me that they feel vulnerable; they fear danger—not from the land, but from men. They fear violence and never quite forget about its most disturbing expression: rape.

Not every woman agrees to live by these constraints and fears. There are women mountaineers and Outward Bound instructors, ranchers and farmers, naturalists and field scientists. Women (most commonly in families with no sons) may grow up hunting with their fathers and continue to hunt as adults. We hear from these women in print—these women who feel their vulnerability the least, who are most successful at soloing in the out-of-doors. Their books mirror their active stance, often focusing on adventure and mountaineering, working with the land on ranches or farms, and observing animal behavior.

Teresa Jordan, one of the most eloquent of writers about ranch life, grew up in the Iron Mountain country of Wyoming. She told me that she took for granted playing with boys, working with men, being taught by men: "Urban women listen to me with astonishment, and tell me that they cannot remember a man ever saying anything serious to them as a child."

Jordan saw gender differences, too. She believes: "It is so much easier culturally for women to love the land, to simply be in it rather than to control it. When I played with boys as a child, we rode horses, we played cowboys and Indians or rustlers: the land was backdrop. When I played with girls, the land and animals were central; we didn't just ride horses, we *became* horses." Jordan never feels vulnerable being alone on the land, but she points out that "in any situation, we feel vulnerable if we have less control, less competence." Her youth made her competent.

Other women have been going out into the landscape since they were children; they continue to go to nature, even after their culture warns them away from going alone; they simply do so thoughtfully, taking care in pragmatic ways. Writer and wilderness survival instructor Leslie Ryan notes that it had not occurred to her to be *afraid* in the wilderness, but that "the travel habits which have always felt sensible to me might appear fearful to others or might be gender specific." Even for a weekend walk in the Rattlesnake Wilderness of western Montana:

> *I leave an itinerary with a friend. At the trailhead, I wait to strike out until there are no men coming or going, and if I meet a man on the mainstretch and he speaks, I outright lie: I say a friend is waiting up the way or fabricate a story about a peak far from my intended path. As soon as it's feasible, I take to the ridge, where voices and footsteps are audible from a distance and the periphery widens. I carry water so there will be no need to recross a trail for replenishment during my stay, and when night falls I turn in, not desiring a telling rim of light around me in the dark.*

Appalachian nature writer Marcia Bonta writes of her childhood passion for the out-of-doors, a passion nurtured by her father and allowed by her more traditional mother, who had another daughter on whom to focus her domestic dreams. Still, "because of my gender," Bonta admits to always taking suitable companions with her to the wilds rather than going alone. As an adult, she and her family settled on five hundred acres of woods in Pennsylvania: "Such a place has allowed me the kind of freedom from fear that remains an impossible dream for most women."

I, too, try to pull off the road to camp in my truck where no one will notice. Friends have suggested that I carry a pistol in my glove box when I am doing fieldwork, but I want no part of guns. Since I am not a seasoned urban dweller, cities can make me feel vulnerable. I feel safer on a rocky ledge halfway up a mountain in the middle of nowhere than I do parking on a dark street in San Francisco to dine in a fine restaurant. But my wife notes the difference between men and women in such situations: I walk out to the truck after dinner and stop to fumble for my keys when I get there; a woman has her keys out and ready and her senses alert for warning signals.

I may be defenseless, but I am male, and by definition that makes me a less approachable target. As a man, whether or not I can quite understand, I must accept the facts that so many women express to me: the vulnerability that seems a constant, a given; the avoidance or management of situations where they feel at risk.

Rape and violence are more urban than rural; indeed, in 1990 the majority of all rapes reported in the United States occurred in the victim's home, in the morning. Women know the rapist in almost 80 percent of all sexual assaults. One out of four women in the United States will be raped sometime in her life.

Leslie Ryan writes of how the existence of rape "undermines trust," creating suspicion that blocks the expression of love and tenderness and innocence. Both the decision to love and the belief in one's safety in wild country are acts of faith. To commit to either requires the most delicate balance of wariness and boldness of which humans are capable. Once again, our best hope lies in helping to teach our children somehow to combine masculine and feminine, integrating sensitivity and strength, turning to the earth as a setting and source for both.

11

To believe that we matter simply because we exist is yet another critical act of faith. Such self-esteem depends on feeling worthwhile and feeling lovable—the "self-love" promoted by a hundred best-selling pop psychology books. People do not always offer dependable reinforcement for our worth, while our peers, our failures, our culture, and far too often, our parents, constantly challenge our self-esteem. One of our first relationships, and one of the most sustaining, can be a relationship with the earth—one built on trust and understanding, leading to comfort.

Jean Baker Miller notes that women, relegated to what men have defined as the "'lesser task' of helping other human beings to develop," have acquired as an unintentional by-product "greater recognition of the essential cooperative nature of human existence." This predisposes women to think like ecologists, to "think like a mountain," in naturalist Aldo Leopold's words.

A tie to nature (as observer rather than conqueror) can create the sweet moments of connection between creatures celebrated by natural history writers. These small epiphanies can increase a child's chances for positive relationships by teaching about intimacy. The land can empower by providing neutral ground for leadership. The earth allows children to be themselves, to be active rather than passive, to take control of their play, their time, their imaginations. These possibilities break through some of the walls built around us by gender roles.

Miller emphasizes that a search for independence—without reference to interaction—has built-in limits. She proposes instead to "include the ability to engage in interactions which empower others and, simultaneously, oneself" as "criteria for maturity"—"to use connections to enhance strength—and strength to enhance connections." We can wish for more men capable of intimate communication and more women who glory in their accomplishments and independence, but before such growth is possible, the bedrock of self-esteem must stand solid. The land can help.

In the United States, despite a generation of efforts at blunting sex-role stereotypes, masculinity generally still centers on "individuation" and separation from one's mother. Femininity remains tied to attachment and social interaction, as psychologist Carol Gilligan outlines in her book, *In a Different Voice*. This is an emotionally charged and polarized field of research, and there are retorts and rebuttals to Gilligan's work in the literature. Biologists remind us that genes and hormones will always influence gender behavior. But the fact is that most parents automatically reinforce boys for going out alone to collect feathers or dig for worms; some are still taken aback when their daughters wish to do the same.

As children assert their independence, parents try to maintain a fragile balance between allowing freedom and setting limits. Everyone involved frequently bumps up against frustrations. Negotiation follows. Parents trust their intuition when they search for a comfortable level of control; culture and experience and gender all influence where they set boundaries.

Gilligan notes the threats to self-esteem that young women face in adolescence, as they are socialized into the expected roles of helpmate and caretaker. It seems ironic indeed that girls receive so little reinforcement for climbing trees, digging in gardens, or turning over rocks to look for spiders when, if Gilligan is right, they so need an unbiased anchor for their self-esteem and, when, if Jean Baker Miller is right, they may have a better chance than boys of making sense of their *relationship* to other creatures and to the earth.

————

Children spend an enormous proportion of their lives in school. Planner Robin Moore notes that school playgrounds provide an opportunity both to even out sex differences and to open up paths to interaction with the natural world. Moore helped to redesign an elementary school playground in Berkeley, California, replacing an acre and a half of asphalt with a diverse group of traditional playground swings and bars; structures and sitting areas; and a half-acre of fishing ponds, streams, woods, and meadows.

He found that girls preferred "games" and "being together," activities that led to social interaction on the play equipment (especially the monkey bars) and in small structures in the "natural resource area." Boys favored competitive ball-playing on the remaining asphalt. Moore's conclusion: "Conventional urban schoolyards are one of the most severely sex-differentiating environments in which children grow up in the U.S."

The natural area of the playground saw wider ranges of activities and more mixing of genders. The bare asphalt "generated more conflict and stress (particularly between the sexes), compared to biotic settings which . . . engendered a more harmonious relationship between children of all types." Children of both sexes described what they called "the dirt area": "It's more like a forest than a playground." "It's a very good place. Really quiet. Lots of kids just sit around there and talk." "It's just perfect."

Children have their own rules about sex roles. Robert Paul Smith lists one version in his childhood reminiscence, *"Where did you go?" "Out." "What did you do?" "Nothing."*

Up until, say seven, boys could play hopscotch. Then, the iron door slammed. From there on out, hopscotch was for girls. On my block, no boy could ever, at whatever age, skip rope. Once in a while, a boy could play higher and higher, which was simply two girls holding the skipping rope . . . higher and higher while a boy jumped until he got his foot caught in the rope and fell on his face. Girls could ride boy's bikes, but boys couldn't ride girls' bikes. Girls could play tag, but not leapfrog. (My, we were backward children.) Girls could carry their books in both arms across their bellies, but boys had to carry them in one hand against their sides. Girls could play immies, occasionally, under great conditions of tolerance, but not mumbly-peg— until around fourteen, when boys would let girls do anything, having plans for later that night, under the street lamps.

Natural places subvert these rules, for the activities that take place there do not fit the categories.

Inside the classrooms, the old rules still hold. Educators have noted a consistent, if unintentional, partiality, with teachers asking boys more questions than girls, questions of greater complexity, granting boys more praise for their successes. American schools unconsciously discourage girls from pushing the limits of their intellects and competing head-to-head with boys. These biases increase in junior high—a crucial interval in the journey each child makes through the educational system—and the results linger. In 1987, women made up nearly half the work force but less than 13 percent of scientists and engineers in the United States; from each group of two thousand ninth-grade girls came a single doctorate in science or engineering. Why?

Testing proves what we know to be true, that such statistics reflect differences in education and experience, rather than in innate skill. To change these numbers will require an immense change in understanding, a belief in the value of opening up choices for both sexes, and culture-wide attention to changing childhood experiences.

I could make a case that the reason women reject engineering and science careers is that they find them overly narrow windows on the world. Women may be better than men at seeing the world whole and avoiding rigid compartmentalization in their lives, and this might explain their choice, and, in part, these statistics.

The same gift for seeing in wholes may help to explain the preponderance of male nature essayists. The female perspective may lead away from the classical nature essay and toward a more creative synthesis of human and landscape concerns. Some of the critical literary statements by women about nature come from fiction writers. From Willa Cather and Sarah Orne Jewett to Margaret Atwood, Ursula Le Guin, and Barbara Kingsolver, this is a distinguished tradition.

My reasoning here assumes gender differences: that women are more synthetic and inclusive in their thinking than men, that women are better able to cope with many tasks and ideas at once and therefore are less sympathetic to extreme specialization. I admire generalists and respect those renaissance women who, as writer and scholar Mary Catherine Bateson puts it, "compose" their lives with a complex score. Bateson goes on:

The physical rhythms of reproduction and maturation create sharper discontinuities in womens' lives than in men's, the shifts of puberty and menopause, of pregnancy, birth, and lactation, the mirroring adaptations to the unfolding lives of children, their departures and returns, the ebb and flow of dependency, the birth of grandchildren, the probability of widowhood. As a result, the ability to shift from one preoccupation to another, to divide one's attention, to improvise in new circumstances, has always been important to women.

In our willingness to make gender distinctions, Bateson and I both can be accused of less than liberated language, of maintaining old stereotypes, of rationalization, of perpetuating marginalization. These are horrendously difficult issues to articulate, let alone untangle. But all of us need to wrangle with them—mothers and fathers, educators and planners, feminists and innocents. Families change first. Institutional change comes later.

▲　　▲　　▲　　▲　　▲　　▲　　▲　　▲　　▲

III

"You have a baby boy!" Time: 5:07 P. M., 7 July 1991. Our obstetrician gave me a pair of surgical scissors; I cut the umbilical cord and, in so doing, physiologically separated our son from his mother, forever.

When I picked Jacob up a few moments later and for the first time put him on my shoulder, I felt a surprising and powerful physical sense of familiarity. I had no idea that I would feel so strongly about becoming father to a boy. Where did this emotional response come from? It seemed from the beginning that I knew this son in a way that I can never know my daughter Dory, as close as we are. My reaction had nothing to do with preferring sons to daughters; it had to do with the simple fact that Jacob and I are males and will always share this. Though I try to give all that I know, all that I can, to both my son and daughter, Dory will retain a certain foreignness, a mystery, because she is female.

When Jacob was born, Joanne and I had been learning about being parents for just three years. We have full intentions of raising Dory to think that she can do anything at all, to be unhindered by any stereotypes of her sex. But when Dory was two, she came home from preschool (a relatively forward-thinking parent cooperative) to announce: "Boys can be doctors, girls can be nurses." Where do these destructive old notions come from?

And now we have a girl and a boy. Along came this son, whose gender made me perceive him differently in his first breath. Feminist scholars argue that all reference to gender perpetuates marginalization of women. And yet my children show me that gender exists. Try as we might to be gender-neutral, Dory and Jacob behave in different ways. Parents of school-age children must deal with decisions about dolls and dress-ups, war toys and make-up, little league and pep club, and in no time at all, issues of sexuality.

Dory knows she is a girl. Psychologists state that Jacob will not reach a clear sense of gender identity until two or three years of age. In the years that follow, he will learn that gender is permanent (excluding major anatomical and hormonal restructuring). Researchers document that by age one and a half, toddlers choose toys that fit sex stereotypes (trucks and soldiers for boys versus dolls and their accessories for girls). Whenever we gave one-year-old Jacob a basket of toys passed down from his sister, he sifted through them one by one and chose the red truck every time. (And as parents, since we know he loves trucks, we buy him trucks, verifying his choice.) Once toddlers learn their gender, however, the rigidity of their stereotypes about how boys and girls should play, work, and dress decreases for a time—but for only a short time.

No matter how dedicated the efforts of parents to teach gender-neutral behavior, children from all cultures continue to behave like boys and girls. In anthropologist Melvin Konner's words: "In every corner of the world where children have been studied, boys are rougher and more violent than girls, and the difference begins by toddlerhood." In Western cultures, by age three, boys and girls choose same-sex play groups. This preference increases through the next three years and remains conspicuous until adolescence.

In Dory's preschool class of two-year-olds, children played in parallel groups of two and three, without much concern for gender. The next year, the three-year-old boys swirled in a gang, turning wooden blocks into rifles, pushing and tumbling over each other, racing around the room. The girls retreated to more quiet spaces, playing house, working with art projects, imagining stories about menageries of toy animals and the farms and castles where they lived. Such childhood socialization powerfully affects behavior, perpetuating whatever roles a culture has created for men and women over the centuries.

Genetics and culture interweave as each gender comes to terms with the environment. Boys may start out with a small genetic edge in visual sensitivity. Girls generally acquire language more quickly, but boys are meanwhile practicing and honing their manual skills, physically manipulating their world far more than girls. Most boys catch up to girls verbally, but once children reach adolescence, American girls typically never catch up to boys in spatial competence (perceptions of the relationships of objects that determine our understanding of place, as tested by working with models and maps). Remember, though, that we build all our cultural biases into experimental design: in Eskimo culture, both girls and boys accompany their fathers on extensive hunting trips, and both sexes perform equally well on spatial tests.

Roger Hart studied what he called "the geography of childhood" in a small New England town in the early 1970s. He found that boys were allowed to range freely more than twice as far away from home as girls in all grades. In fourth grade, as children took on their first jobs, the boys delivered papers and mowed lawns, learning the lay of the town; girls hired out as babysitters. Boys broke their parents's rules about boundaries more than girls, and Hart perceived an implicit message in the parents's behavior: "'Boys will be boys,' meaning that we must expect them to explore more, engage in more rough play, be more physically active, and even get into trouble more, but that they must expect punishment when caught. Such are the attitudes toward the making of a man."

Hart and his co-researcher Susan Saegert summarize the depressing and inevitable result of such control of girls: "Not only is environmental exploration and freedom denied to them, but also their confidence and ability to cope with environmental matters are likely to be undermined." They liken the boy's experience to the "experimentation and self-directed learning" of the driver of a car, the girl's, to the passenger's, who can only "suggest and observe."

Middle childhood, when so much of cultural learning takes place, lasts from about the age of six, when the brain develops fully, until the beginning of adolescence. For boys, this crucial interlude may last a full two years longer—40 percent longer—than for girls, for whom puberty comes two years earlier on average, ending "the wonder years," the magical human interval of general receptivity. In the conventional pattern, while boys continue to have the freedom to learn and explore the environment around them, girls are moving on into self-involvement and preparation for adult sexual roles. British psychologist M. H. Matthews concludes that girls' "environmental behaviour tends to be restrained by the social mores of their parents, teachers and peers."

Adolescent girls throughout the world typically stay close to home, interacting with their mothers and other adult females. They may develop rich relationships with the land, but these most often come from a relatively restricted circle around home, and social experiences within that circle: gathering plants with a group of women, tending a garden with other women. Gardens, in fact, were the key to understanding the frontier American woman, according to historian Annette Kolodny: "while men sought new Edens . . . altering the landscape to make it comply with their dreams . . . women . . . cultivated small gardens in order 'to render Home a Paradise.'"

Boys, in Melvin Konner's words, "do *not* have comparable contact with their fathers, or in fact with adults of either sex. So they gravitate after puberty to other boys, forming all-male youth groups that take them farther from home and draw them into competition and aggression." The ideal of a young man apprenticing to a wise elder sets apart a small elite.

This contrast between genders, nearly universal, explains some of the struggles women undergo when breaking into men's professional networks. The men have been practicing one-upsmanship since childhood; the women, in turn, have been working cooperatively all their lives.

Gender differences can contribute to a valuable diversity of vision. The historic constructs of femininity and masculinity in American culture are something else entirely, clearly in need of revision. Today, we have more freedom to break out of these stereotypes than in more traditional cultures. Paradoxically, women living in conventional Western urban culture are more alienated from the land than similar women in traditional cultures. They have farther to go to claim their own land, though with their educations and freedom they have more fuel for the journey.

As feminist scholarship evolved, writers noted that the set of values which led individuals and cultures to devalue women led them to treat the land in the same destructive fashion. Clearly, to change this, we need to raise daughters and sons who value the earth and all its people. As Jean Baker Miller reiterates: "the areas designated as women's place are *not* secondary or unimportant. . . . We have reached the end of the road that is built on the set of traits held out for male identity—advance at any cost, pay any price, drive out all competitors, and kill them if necessary. . . . we have arrived at a point from which we must seek a basis of faith in connection—and not only faith but recognition that it is a requirement for the existence of human beings."

We need men who value the strengths of affiliation and relationship and connection and who choose not to use their power to dominate and develop the last imperiled natural environments of our planet. We need women who defy convention and act as role models for girls inhibited by the old norms. We need to write books about such women, insert them in television series, infiltrate the culture with their strength. Women will never achieve equity without such changes in values. The earth will not flourish, and may not survive, without such changes in values— values formed in childhood.

I wish for my son and daughter the opportunity and courage to pursue whatever their dreams might be. My son will have the advantages of his gender in making his way in the world. My daughter will need extra strength to fulfill her dreams.

Dory is a powerful emotional presence now. I hope that she preserves that power. I believe this is possible, but I know that she will have her struggles. As a parent, simply knowing that fact can help me to pay attention to her needs. Girls need an extra dose of bravery to overcome cultural stereotypes. Anything we can do to maintain her self-esteem will help. Jacob, too, will need a strong sense of self—to allow him the freedom to modify old ways, to range beyond male stereotypes and yet still feel intact.

My own anchor of strength in hard times has always been the land. In the details and distinctness of nature I find solace and clarity. I rest in the sun to heal. I hope the earth can serve as powerfully for my children. All I can do is to create opportunities for that to happen—lots of opportunities, safe ones, programmed for success—and then stand back and let the earth do its work. If my children choose other anchors, I must remember that this is not because of my failures but rather testimony to their independence, to their freedom to follow their own passions.

The advantages of strong people, strong women, in wild places as well as in cities, seep into every corner of our lives. For ourselves, and for our planet, we must be both strong and strongly connected—with each other, with the earth. As children, we need time to wander, to be outside, to nibble on icicles and watch ants, to build with dirt and sticks in a hollow of the earth, to lie back and contemplate clouds and chickadees. These simple acts forge the connections that define a land of one's own— home and refuge for both girls and boys. Mentors help, answering the questions we bring back from the land. With these childhood experiences we begin. They form the secure foundation to which we return again and again in our struggle to be strong *and* connected, to be complete.

S.T.

Children in Touch,
Creatures in Story

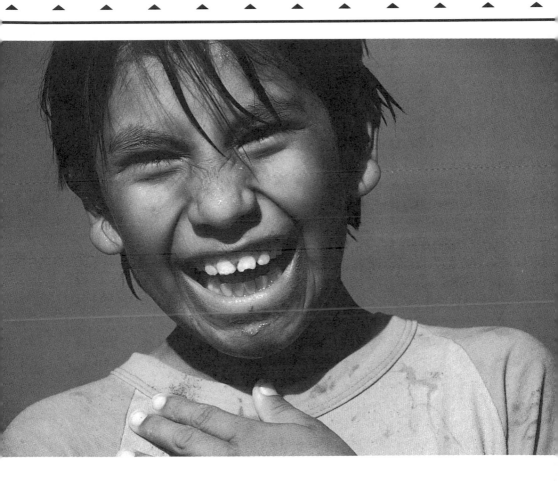

▲ ▲ ▲ ▲ ▲ ▲ ▲ ▲ ▲

W̲e were gathered together for the New Year, friends and members of an extended family on a Mexican ranch, tucked back into a desert valley three hours south of the U.S. border. The elderly grandmother—of Mayo Indian blood—kept all the women busy sorting and cooking beans, stuffing tamales, and patting out tortillas. Her husband, a Sonoran mestizo cowboy, was not too old to do hard work, but that week he let his sons and sons-in-law do most of the wrangling, wood-cutting, and hay-hauling; he simply guided them, quietly, through the tasks at hand.

When chores were done, the adults had little else to do. And so, while we drank coffee, pinole, and chocolate, and watched a pack of two dozen children run wild through the house, ranch yard, and desert, stories were told.

Because the nights were long, and the ranch without electricity, a bonfire was lit just before dusk. Family and guests would hunker around it for several hours after dark, nursing more hot drinks, roasting marshmallows, and swapping tales.

The preparation for the bonfire ritual would begin several hours earlier. Around three in the afternoon, the grandmother, tired of children darting in and out of the kitchen where she was preparing dinner, would wipe her hands on her apron, walk outside, clap her hands, and start giving commands: "Stay out of the house now, you little ones! You two, climb down from that tree! The rest of you, come down off the haystack, and get over here! I need your help! It's going to be cold and windy tonight! We need extra wood for the bonfire! *Andeles*, get going for some wood, enough wood to keep us all warm!" She feigns a shiver in her sweater and long dress, then dispatches all the children to the desert surrounding the ranch yard.

Suddenly filled with purpose, the older adolescents quickly organize the troops—right down to the three- and four-year-olds—and march them out the wooden gate, into open country. With one other parent, I straggle along behind them. We usually keep within earshot, but the children pay us no mind as they ramble and playfully argue their way through the desert scrub.

I soon realize that I am witness to the most comprehensive environmental education lesson I have ever seen presented. Geography, plant ecology, hydrology, archaeology, history, and ethnobotany are all wrapped into one roving seminar, offered impromptu by a team of field instructors, none of them over fourteen years of age. As the children gather kindling over the next hour and a half, they also accumulate knowledge and stories about their grandparents' ranch.

"Where can we get enough wood?" one girl visiting from a city in Baja California asks her country cousins. "There are hardly any sticks nearby the house anymore."

"That's because Grandma gets her wood nearby the house during the times when we're not around to help her. We have to go farther away to get what we need today, maybe over there where Grandpa built their first adobe house."

"No, that wasn't their *first* house. He made one out of mud and sticks when they first came to the ranch a real long time ago. It's over by those dead trees—that's where the first well went dry, so they had to move."

"I've never seen an empty well," one little boy cries. "Let's go over there!"

"Why not? Maybe some branches have fallen down off those old trees." They are off, like a herd of goats seeking palatable forage.

A few minutes later, each child is busy looking for a branch he or she can drag or carry away. The local ruffians-in-residence direct their city cousins toward deadfalls of mesquite, and caution them against the remains of a eucalyptus tree. "That wood is no good, it's too smelly. It makes the bonfire stink like medicine."

"Yeah, mesquite or ironwood are better. Mesquite smoke is sweet. And you can always tell the ironwood, even when there is just one piece left by itself on the ground. It weighs a ton."

"Let's show them that place where the old chunks of ironwood sit on the ground like rocks. It's over there, at the bottom of that rocky *bajada*."

Suddenly, the herd veers off course, farther away from the house, over a small rise, and down the slope. There, where the slope meets a small sandy wash, the children find fossilized fragments of ironwood chunks, and pot shards as well.

"Grandpa says that these are from water *ollas* that Indian ladies used to balance on their heads, no hands, like the way I can ride my bike."

"You ride your bike with clay pots of water on your head? No wonder all this pottery is broken!" one of the older kids teases.

"No, I didn't break the potteries. The ladies carried them no hands, like the way I ride my bike. Except I'm better. I never drop a thing."

The smaller kids go ahead with one of the older girls, back toward the ranch house; when the boys are done teasing each other, they run to catch up with the rest of the mob. They notice that one child is dragging along a bright red spray of branches. "Where did you get that?"

The child points. "From that bush by the side of the wash."

"That's *yerba de la flecha*, it's poison. The Indians used it to poison arrows and fish. I don't think it's good to burn." The child shrugs, drops the branch, and picks up another under a mesquite tree. Everyone heads into the ranch yard, as the sun goes down behind our backs.

There, under the supervision of parents and uncles, the children sort the wood: *palo verde* and small kindling for heating tortillas on the *comal*; mesquite for the bonfire; and ironwood set aside for the moment. As the boys stack the wood in piles, they ask their grandfather when he built the different houses on the ranch, and why he located them where he did; one of the girls approaches her grandmother and whispers, "Nana, what kind of Indians used the poisons in that *yerba de la flecha*?"

"Who knows? Apaches or Seris, I guess."

"What did *your* people do with it?" she whispers.

"Well," the grandmother sighs, "it's been many years . . . but I remember that when I was a girl, my uncle would gather little white cocoons off the stems of the *yerba de la flecha*. I would help him. He called them *teneboi'im*. He was a *pascola* dancer—you have seen them, haven't you? They, like the deer dancers, wear hundreds of these cocoons tied around their ankles, and they make a rhythm as they dance. I grew up with that sound."

The stories for the night have been set in place: we hear about the grandmother growing up in southern Sonora, moving to the new ranch as a young bride, and helping her husband build a house to begin a new life. The children listen wide-eyed, as the stories touch down in the places they romped through just that afternoon. Abandoned houses become homes again, as the family remembers its origins. And as the elders share their memories lodged in the surrounding country, the family renews its membership in the land.

What I witnessed among those children is nothing unique to Indians, Mexicans, ranch families, or desert dwellers. The playful exploration of habitat by cohorts of children—as well as the gradual accumulation of an oral tradition about the land—have been essential to child development for over a million years, as the emergence of language allowed the telling of stories and an expression of kinships with the earth. Through such informal means, tens of thousands of generations of children have become ecologically literate about their home ground. They have gradually learned hundreds of specific guidelines and rules about how to respond to particular plants and animals, not only the ones with which they had frequent contact, but seldom seen, mythic ones as well. The qualities of firewoods, the songs of birds, the identities of floral fragrances and mammalian musks have all filtered into their consciousness.

This was what *environmental education* was like before indigenous children were pulled out of their homes to go to boarding schools in distant lands; before *environment* was partitioned off as a concern distinct from that of simply learning to live well with the "others"—the other-than-human creatures—around you. *Story* had not yet been sequestered in books, nor had pertinent knowledge about the natural world been reduced to "facts" ritually presented only by the members of a scientific priesthood.

Southwest Indian storyteller Leslie Silko has reminded us that considerable biological knowledge is embodied in oral narratives, for most land-based cultures perceive "the world and themselves within that world as part of a continuous story composed of innumerable bundles of stories. . . . Thus stories about the Creation and Emergence of human beings and animals into this world continue to be retold. . . . Accounts of the appearance of the first Europeans . . . were no more or less important than stories about the biggest mule deer ever taken, or adulterous couples surprised in cornfields and chicken coops."

Such stories were not merely intended for adult ears, nor were they turned into innocuous "fables" sanitized and simplified for the sake of children. Silko observes that "everyone, from the youngest child to the oldest person, was expected to listen and be able to recall or tell a portion, if only a small detail, from a narrative account or story. Thus the remembering and retelling were a communal process. Even if a key figure, an elder who knew much more than others, were to die unexpectedly, the system would remain intact."

When children encountered unfamiliar plants and animals, the stories informed them of the roles these beings played in their culture. Unlike our own society's preoccupation with charismatic wildlife, such stories were not restricted to cuddly, big-eyed creatures and frightening predators. For instance, my Yaqui and Mayo neighbors still fill their oral literature with more than twenty-nine kinds of plants, thirteen invertebrates, eighteen birds, twenty-seven mammals, and fourteen kinds of fish, reptiles, and amphibians. Only a tenth of these nonhuman beings of Mayo and Yaqui stories are domesticated—these being the tamed livestock and cultivated crops that the Yaqui and Mayo have tended. More than 90 percent of the characters in their stories, songs, and speeches are wild plants and creatures that predate agriculture as part of Yaqui existence in the *huya ania*, or "wilderness world."

Traditionally, expression in a native tongue depended upon familiarity with those plant and animal characters. To be lazy or lascivious like a coyote, to stand firm like a stalwart saguaro cactus, to be distant and uncontrollable like a mountain sheep—these qualities provided the metaphors through which human behavior was placed into perspective. The images absorbed from one's surroundings also became means of self-expression.

I once happened to call upon an elderly O'odham friend just as he was returning from hunting a mockingbird.

"Are you going to eat its meat, or use its feathers?" I asked naively.

"No, it's not for me," my friend said in a tone tinged with sadness and solemnity. He was quiet for a while, and I sensed that he was about to tell me something that was difficult for him to explain. "It's for my grandson, the one who has never said anything. I have to skin this bird, and cook it up for him, to help him so that he can begin to talk. You know, those mockingbirds talk a lot."

It is as if one must ingest the world—the wildness, the *animal* within it—in order to overcome the prelingual barrier to expression. The loquacious mockingbird, for the O'odham, had become a sacrament embodying this connection.

There are still many children in this world who live where they have primary contact with wild nature; who still hear the old stories; and who have uncles and grandfathers or grandmothers and aunts to guide them through their gender's rites of passage. Yet the percentage of children who have frequent exposure to wildlands and to other, undomesticated species is smaller than ever before in human history.

The traditions of animal stories and rites of initiation in the wild have gradually declined over many generations in northern Europe, urban America, the far East, and the Mediterranean. However, the rupture of such traditions has been far more rapid and severe in native North America, South America, Africa, and the Australian outback. Since World War II, television, formal classroom education, and urban migration have dramatically disrupted oral traditions, and reduced the frequency of most children's involvement with other-than-human organisms. There has been a greater intergenerational atrophy of such traditions among indigenous peoples during the last three decades than ever before. While their communities may not immediately recognize the severity of this loss of orally transmitted knowledge about the natural world, the consequences are perilous, for once the reservoirs of folklore have been dissipated, it is increasingly hard to replenish them.

Fundamental to this cultural loss is the phenomenon Robert Michael Pyle has termed "the extinction of experience," or the termination of direct, frequent contact between children and wildlife. While many children may visit zoos, watch nature films, or cuddle with pets and stuffed animals, their responses to other species have become more "politically correct" but less grounded on their own visceral experiences.

Studies have demonstrated that such a vicarious view of nature has developed among urban, suburban, and even some rural black and white children in parts of the United States. These studies prompted me to explore whether such a devastating trend has yet reached into the rural cultures of the desert Southwest where I live. After informally interviewing dozens of Mexican and Indian children during the winter and spring of 1992, I began to see that such trends were indeed evident among some of the desert-dwelling populations of southern Arizona. But why, I wondered, had they become evident even among the children who lived in or near wild places, in communities where at least some of the elders still knew ancient stories and songs about animals and plants?

Concerned that profound shifts had begun in the way children were growing up in the desert, I decided to listen to what was going on among the kids who seemed to be the most likely of any I had encountered to sustain their involvement with nature and ancient cultural traditions. I could not have found anyone better suited to help me with this task than Sara St. Antoine. Sara is an accomplished writer of children's novels and of environmental education curricula. Her graduate work at the Yale School of Forestry and Environmental Studies was under the guidance of Steve Kellert, who pioneered "wildlife attitude surveys" among children and adults in five countries around the world. Sara is familiar with this brand of environmental sociology and sensitive to children of all colors and all ages.

Together, we interviewed fifty-two Anglo, Hispanic, O'odham, and Yoeme (Yaqui/Mayo) children during the summer of 1992, in towns such as Sonoyta and Quitovac, Sonora, and Ajo, Avra Valley, and Marana, Arizona. The majority of the children lived beyond the reaches of big cities such as Tucson, and in the shadows of two U.S. National Parks and one Mexican protected zone in the desert. Although all those children interviewed were between eight and fourteen years of age, and spoke either English or Spanish as their first language, many of the Indian children lived in households where their grandparents spoke a Native American language as well as a European one.

Sara and I were amazed at the range of environmental education opportunities available to most of the children we encountered, and were heartened by the depth of concern that many had for the conservation of endangered plants, wildlife, and habitat. Nearly all of them had visited national parks, zoos, outdoor natural history museums, or botanical gardens. Most had read books about plants and animals, or had seen films about their increasing rarity and their need for protection.

Most of the children did claim some direct and pleasurable interaction with desert landscapes and their organisms—either through plant gathering, playful capture of small animals, or pursuit of larger ones. Nevertheless, the vast majority of the children we interviewed were now gaining most of their knowledge about other organisms vicariously. The trends were staggering: 77 percent of the Mexican kids, 61 percent of the Anglo, 60

percent of the Yaqui, and 35 percent of the O'odham kids felt
that they had seen more animals on television and in movies than
they had personally seen in the wild. These local trends mirror
results from a 1992 survey of fifth and sixth graders in the United
States, in which 53 percent of the children listed the media as
their primary teacher about the environment; 31 percent reo-
ported that they learned more about the environment from
school, and only 9 per cent claimed they obtained most of their
environmental information at home and in the wild.

Roughly half of the children we interviewed felt that they now
learn more about the desert flora and wildlife from books than
from their elders. But Alvron, a Mexican-American boy from a
small Arizona town, epitomizes the modern dilemma. When
asked whether his family or his books were the primary source of
what he knew about animals, his answer was immediate: "Neither. The Discover Channel!"

Alvron may have been more unabashed in his admission of this
preference than others in his cohort of kids, but they had the
same fatal attraction to television. Only the children in the poorest, most remote desert communities—where television recep-
tion is also the poorest—spent less time after school watching
TV than playing outside or listening to stories from their elders.

Some would argue that if the "ultimate message" of various
kinds of instruction is the same—in this case, respect for
nature—then it makes little difference whether children get the
message via television, books, museum exhibits, stories from
elders, or from personal encounters. However, Native American
educators Ernie Lennie and Barbara Smith have taken issue with
this claim. Lennie says that "the type of learning we get in
school and also on TV is the type where we just sit and absorb.
But in family life . . . children learn directly from their parents.
Learning has to come from doing."

The experience of Inuit people living to the north of Lennie's

Canadian homeland underscores Lennie's hypothesis. In certain Inuit communities, the impairment to vision known as *myopia* became commonplace within the first generation exposed to books and audiovisual media in the schools. Inuit children were seldom diagnosed for myopia earlier in this century, even though it is now suspected that they have a genetic predisposition to this eye condition. And yet, when Inuit children took to staring at books and TV sets, myopia increased to affect more than half of school-age children. No longer exercising their eyesight to read the rich and subtle landscapes of the north country, they did not receive the visual stimuli required to fully develop their eyes during critical stages in their early development. It is a sad irony of formal education that it may turn an entire native people "shortsighted" within a matter of years.

Contrast the tendency toward short-sightedness among young Inuit with the astonishing visual abilities of their traditional forebears, testified by the maps and stories collected by Barry Lopez in *Arctic Dreams*, and by Edmund Carpenter in *Eskimo Realities*. Carpenter has written that the traditional Inuit,

> . . . as observers, in both detail and precision . . . continually amazed me. Again and again, they saw what I did not. A seal on the ice was known to them long before I could see it, even when the direction was indicated. Yet my eyes are 20-20. Standing at the floe edge they could tell at a glance whether it was bird or seal, seal or square-flipper. They shout "tingmisut!" (plane) usually long before I could see anything and the children would continue to watch long after it had disappeared from my view . . .

Today's Inuit children may not only have less access to the wild animals which sustained their forebears; they may actually be losing their very ability to see them as their ancestors did.

Sara felt that the desert children we interviewed seemed to

have as much access to wild open spaces as any children she had ever met, and greater exposure to traditional hunting and gathering as well. She guessed that the frequency of TV-dominated wildlife watchers would be even higher if we had included more urban dwellers in our samples. Yet despite *access* to open spaces, few of these children were spending much time alone in nature. When asked if they had ever spent even a half-hour alone in a wild place, none of the Yaqui children, 42 percent of the O'odham, 47 percent of the Anglos, and only 39 percent of the Mexican kids responded positively.

The kind of solitude in nature that historically instilled a sense of wonder in many incipient naturalists was shared only by a few of the kids interviewed. For a rare few, however, being out in the desert was not the same as being *alone*. A young girl from Ajo, Arizona, was confused by my question when I asked if she had ever been alone in the desert for more than a half-hour's time.

"No . . . well, yes, maybe, well, what do you mean?" she asked me. "Do you mean I'm completely alone?"

I was confused by her vacillation, until she mentioned that she loves to take a riding trail into the desert at least a couple afternoons after school every week. "See, I ride out into the desert on my horse, and we stop to watch the sunset together. . . . I don't ever really feel alone, because my horse is there with me." That sensibility—that the presence of other creatures can keep one from feeling lonely or isolated—is apparently becoming a scarce commodity among children today.

Their lack of solitude in nature made us curious about other outdoor activities that kids often do together, pursuits that may lead a child into later study of natural history: the casual collection of feathers, bones, butterflies, and beautiful stones, not so much for analysis as for play. Paleontologist David Steadman has remembered his own roots as a naturalist, saying that, every summer, he and his brothers would roam the woods and farmlands, turning over logs to see what was hiding there, catching turtles, and picking up bones. He mused that after twenty years of formal education, and three degrees, he is now paid to do what he loved to do as a child.

Again, we were surprised that a significant percentage of kids today are not collecting, carrying around, or keeping such natural treasures as nearly all children have done throughout history. Thirty-five percent of the O'odham, 60 percent of the Yaqui, 44 percent of the Mexican, and 46 percent of the Anglo children have *never* been involved in such a pursuit. While some protectionists might be relieved that we found fewer children hunting or trapping animals, or taking natural curiosities out of their habitats, this diminished hands-on involvement with nature is strongly correlated with diminished sensory and intellectual engagement with their biological environment.

What most disturbed us was that many kids know few of the basic facts about the desert that can only be learned first-hand and not through the media. Some of these failures would have been unimaginable a century ago: for example, 55 percent of the Mexican kids we interviewed didn't know you can eat prickly pear fruit, a food that has been a staple in northern Mexico for more than eight thousand years. Roughly a quarter of the Indian kids weren't sure whether the aromatic creosote bush, known to them as "greasewood," smelled stronger after rains than cactus did, even though older generations of Indians claimed that creosote gave their homeland its distinctive smell. Nearly a fifth of all kids interviewed could not recall that desert birds sing more actively early in the morning than at midday.

Perhaps these figures are not so unexpected, considering that over 60 percent of the children we talked with say that they learn more about plants and animals at school than at home—knowledge about nature is thought to be gained through formal education more than from personal observation. Yet classroom, museum, and park education programs are not the problem; they simply can't enrich kids who don't have much personal experience in nature on which to build. The kids who scored highest on factual questions in our survey inevitably had informal interactions with desert plants and animals that whetted their curiosity for classroom and museum studies. A good teacher or nature guide can nurture such incipient naturalists, but they can seldom create them from scratch.

How is it then, that a classroom teacher or nature center guide can hope to nurture young naturalists? Tohono O'odham Nation education director Rosilda Manual once said to me, "For a long time, whenever I heard someone talking about environmental education, I thought they were just wanting to upgrade science education about the environment. Then last year, I realized that environmental education can be *cultural* education too. I was fortunate to grow up with a grandfather who taught me to respect other ways of life, those of animals, plants, Whites, Blacks, other Indians. He taught me that we have a special way of looking at the world, but others do as well."

I have become concerned that formal education unintentionally leads to discounting what can be learned at home, especially when traditional knowledge is juxtaposed with that presented in texts by authoritative science experts. Most desert children claim that they have learned more about plants and animals from school than their grandparents had learned their entire lives. Why? Perhaps most of the students know that their grandparents had not finished as many years in school as had they or their teachers, so they were obviously not as "smart." I was especially saddened to learn that 58 percent of the O'odham and 60 percent of the Yaqui kids felt this way, because their grandparents have taught me the most valuable information about the desert I know.

Sara noticed that by contrast only 38 percent of the Anglo-American children felt they knew more about plants and animals than their parents and grandparents did. A higher percentage of the Anglos had completed their formal education, so their children perhaps perceived that they knew more because of that. Sara reasoned that there may not have been such a large intergenerational difference in Anglo education as there was for the Indian children we interviewed and their parents. Still, I was most struck by the idea that all the detailed knowledge of the plants and animals held by Indian elders was not considered valuable exactly because it was *not* book learning! It was as though our society's high regard for zoological or botanical "facts" derived from lab experiments, books, and science films has invalidated knowledge learned by other means.

And yet, as Barbara Smith notes, there is something that makes narrative stories from elders a particularly effective means for transmitting values as well as knowledge regarding the natural world. Thinking in particular of the way she had absorbed Dine legends from her elders in Canada's Northwest Territories, Smith observes, "Legends are tools that help people grow in certain ways. A lot of what matters is the power and the feeling of the experience." She adds that "when you find something in a museum, or even on TV, you can see it alright, but you're really looking only at the shell."

Yaqui Indian educator Felipe Molina also feels that values can be taught through traditional stories in ways that school science classes do not presently offer. "When I was in school, we learned about plants in science," Felipe told Sara outside his home in Yoeme village. "We learned how to name their parts or how they grow, but we never went the next step, which was to talk about how to *care* for them." This added dimension is one that Yaqui lore could offer to children at home, or even through bringing elders into the schools. However, until recently, Felipe has observed that Yaqui legends have never been "uplifted" or given credence in the schools.

Such realizations are not unique to Native Americans. Halfway around the world, the great Italian novelist and naturalist Italo Calvino grew up in a world where his father taught him that each tree and each bird has a story to tell. Calvino once wrote that "new knowledge does not compensate for the knowledge spread only by direct oral transmission, which, once lost, cannot be regained or retransmitted: no book can teach what can be learned only in childhood if you lend an alert ear and eye to the song and flight of birds or if you find someone who knows how to give them a specific name."

Our world today is one in which we are losing ways of speaking about plants and animals as rapidly as we are losing endangered species themselves. Oral traditions about plants, animals, treacherous waters, and complex topography depend upon specific vocabularies that encode particularities which may not be recognized in the lexicons of commonly spoken, widespread languages. As half of the two hundred native languages in North America die when their last elder speakers fall silent, thousands of Indian children will have forfeited the chance to speak of their plant and animal neighbors in ways filled with the nuances of feeling that characterized their forebears' speech.

Native American poet-linguist Nora Dauenhauer has reminded us that language extinction is "forever," just as much as the loss of species is irrevocable: "If a Native American language dies, there is no place on earth one can travel to learn it. The public statements that some school administrators continue to make in opposition to teaching native languages would not be tolerated if made about some endangered species of bird or snail."

Sara and I wondered if even the most fundamental knowledge about common plants and animals was still being orally transmitted to O'odham and Yaqui children through their aboriginal language. She pasted together a picture book of desert plants and animals, which we first showed to the Yaqui and O'odham children, and then to their parents and grandparents. We simply asked them all to name in their native dialect the various organisms illustrated in the makeshift booklet.

Most of the children bowed out before naming even a single creature in their forebearers' tongue; they had not grown up speaking anything but English or Spanish or, in a few cases, were too shy to do so in front of strangers. But the dozen children who did try to name the seventeen native species shown in the drawings averaged barely five correct names. In contrast, their grandparents averaged about fifteen native names for the seventeen drawings. The younger generation knew less than a third of the plant and animal names that their elders knew, and even less of the lore associated with them.

It was not just the children who knew little of their native language; most of their parents under forty had the same difficulty remembering plant and animal names. The ones who had known me from earlier visits with the elders remembered from past discussions that I spoke some O'odham. When a name escaped both the children and the young parents, they would ask *me* to remind them of the native term. Even though I had never gained more than a rudimentary grasp of O'odham terms for crops and wildlife—perhaps no more than a five-year-old might have known a century ago—it dawned on me that Indians my own age possibly knew fewer of these native terms than I did.

But why should they be familiar with these terms? Despite the vestiges of traditional instruction persisting in many Native American communities, Indians of my own generation have been barraged by the same messages from television, radio, schoolbooks and federally mandated classroom curricula as I. We were all brought up being subtly told by the world outside of our own families and cultures that our traditional knowledge was not worth that much; if the words our relatives used for certain birds, weeds, or foods were not in a dictionary, they probably didn't matter.

Nevertheless, part of what once made my O'odham and Yaqui-Mayo neighbors unique is that their food as well as their stories were all in some way derived from the desert. No wonder the Tohono O'odham tribe of southern Arizona refers to itself in English simply as "the Desert People;" their very blood, muscles, and minds were literally made of molecules from desert seeds, desert meat, desert earth. Today, however, their molecules have nearly the same elements in them as mine: beef from Monfort's feedlots in Colorado; winter apples shipped from Puerto Montt in Chile; potatos mass-produced by a Mormon million-aire in Idaho.

The very plants and animals upon which the O'odham once depended are now increasingly out of sight and out of mind. Robert Michael Pyle elaborates on the "cycle of disaffection" that is triggered by the extinction of experience: "as cities and metastasizing suburbs forsake their natural diversity, and their citizens grow more removed from personal contact with nature, awareness and appreciation retreat. This breeds apathy toward environmental concerns and, inevitably, further degradation of common habitat . . . [leading to] the total loss of rarities. People who care, conserve; people who don't know, don't care. What is the extinction of the condor to a child who has never seen a wren?"

If fables about animals are forgotten, it does not necessarily follow that the animals themselves cease to exist. Nevertheless, as floral and faunal narratives play less of a role in keeping us alert to the fate of other biota, we are more likely to let their existence slip through our fingers without ever noticing this loss.

What can be done to break this vicious cycle of disaffection? As Sara and I drove back from our interviews with the children of Quitovac, Ajo, Marana, and Sonoyta, we deliberated on this dilemma.

Could better funding for environmental education programs in outdoor museums and parks fit the bill? Certainly, such programs are valuable, for they move children beyond the classroom. And yet, those in existence remain miserably underfunded. At the same time, making them bigger will not always be better. The public gardens and zoos that pump tens of thousands of students down their trails do not always quench the thirst for intimate contact. Neither do the computer games and video libraries catering to science and nature themes. The finest environmental educators I know despair that within their institutional frameworks, their own best efforts are being spread too far, too thin. These teachers may pique a child's curiosity for a moment, but they are seldom given the chance to follow through with the child in any deeper experience with nature.

By the end of our summer with desert children, Sara and I had identified three key strategies for staving off the extinction of experience: intimate involvement with plants and animals; direct exposure to a variety of wild animals carrying out their routine behaviors in natural habitats; and teaching by community elders (indigenous or otherwise) about their knowledge of the local biota. Some of these activities are easy for schools, nature centers, and museums to accomodate and sponsor, but others are not.

Sara finally framed the situation in this manner: "Formal education programs cannot make up for, and should not try to replace the spontaneous hands-on experience of nature, nor the richness of intergenerational story-telling." Instead, we agreed, they should incorporate such elements of traditional learning about nature into their programs, so that the amount of time formerly dedicated to such activities is not further usurped.

Some of these strategies already have been implemented to various degrees in classrooms and outdoor education programs across the country. For example, psychiatrist Aaron Katcher has pioneered "therapy through companion animals" in Pennsylvanian schools dedicated to children with learning disabilities such as autism and hyperactivity. He has documented that "dogs, cats, turtles and dolphins have produced speech in autistic children"; that five hours of contact with pets each day "decreased aggression, while increasing peer cooperation and acceptance of responsibility" in children with chronically deficient attention spans.

In discussing the benefits and limitations of so-called "animal therapy," Katcher is candid; some of the children revert to their former behavior as soon as they are removed from contact with the school's animals and are taken home to settings where other animals are absent. In addition, Katcher is among the scholars who do not believe that manageable, domesticated cuddlies and tamed, zoo-kept beasts can offer the same quality of experience that comes from encounters with fully wild animals: "Our responses to pets may be clues to our needs for other, more differentiated animals." Unlike most pet therapy promoters, Katcher's programs provide children with time for bird-watching, fishing, and exposure to untamed or wild animals. Katcher told me that once the kids have been given frequent access to animals, the same behavior changes occur time and time again: "The kids who have the opportunity to visit these animals begin to do so spontaneously. When that happens, their learning skills go up and their disruptive behavior decreases."

Katcher's work suggests that we need not try to do what television does, which is to set up the assumption of immediate intimacy with all animals, even when that cannot be achieved in the field. We need not pretend we are bosom buddies with aloof predators, nor shower all our appreciation on the rare raptor or hyper-intelligent cetacean. Real attention given to a covey of quail, a swarm of termites, a litter of packrats will do for most kids I know.

Peggy Turk-Boyer, who runs the Center for the Study of Deserts and Oceans in northern Mexico, can elicit more sustained engagement from students with a tidepool rich in invertebrates than she can with a school of surf-breaking dolphins. "Small creatures which stay within reach can capture their attention for hours," she has observed, "while their contact with whales or dolphins can only be fleeting."

I have watched other children in Mexico entranced by the industriousness of leaf-cutter ants; I myself could watch these fungus-farmers for hours on end without tiring.

I recall taking my then two- and four-year-old children to a zoo once; that experience cured me of my assumptions about what would impress them. While I tried to steer them toward tapirs and gators—uncaged, but on the other side of ten-foot moats—they spent their time feeding ground squirrels that had "broke into the zoo" to take advantage of the tons of squandered feed. After a while, they discovered one ground squirrel that kept a cache of food under the sidewalk leading toward the "exotic wildlife" area; we sat down and spent the rest of the afternoon engaged in hide-and-seek with this spermophilous visitor to the zoo. No name tag in Latin, no interpretative message about his role in the "chain of life" was needed for this creature to capture the attention and hearts of my escorts for hours.

Once children have seen the behavior of a variety of animals in their natural contexts, it is easier to engage them in balanced discussions of values, ethics, and spiritual responses of humans to the nonhuman world. They tend not to dismiss all predators as evil killers, all scavengers as uncouth, all wide-eyed furry herbivores as benign. Such stereotypes tell us more about ourselves after all than about the animals around us.

In a Salish tale told by tribal storyteller Johnny Moses, we learn that "long ago, the trees thought they were people, long ago, the animals thought they were people . . ." Then he adds, "someday, they will say . . . long ago, the human beings thought *they* were people."

Native American elders served as mentors for Johnny Moses, Rosilda Manual, and Felipe Molina. For Kamau Kambui, however, the abolitionist Harriet Tubman has served as his guide to a world of diversity and human dignity. Trained in social work, recreational therapy, and Outward Bound leadership skills, Kambui has developed and used an Underground Railroad reenactment at Wilder Forest in Minnesota since 1986. Over the years there, various Forest staff members have played the role of Harriet Tubman, who serves as guide to those willing to experience what it feels like to escape slavery by a passage through unknown wilderness.

"The reenactments are as authentic as possible," Kambui claims. "Superman is make-believe," Kambui says to the kids as they decide whether or not they'll go out into the woods after dark, "but Harriet Tubman is real."

The Wilder Forest staff has transformed the traditional nature walk into something far more emotionally rich: "Dogs howl in pursuit; chains rattle as slave catchers close in; and fear spurs the footsteps of slaves as they thrash through the dark forest in desperate attempts to reach freedom."

Nonetheless, the guidance of Harriet Tubman helps pull them through. The original Tubman first escaped the bonds of slavery in 1849, by traveling at night from Maryland to Pennsylvania, using only the North Star and her own cunning as guides. She later made eighteen trips into the South, to help more than three hundred African slaves find food, shelter, and medicine in the wilderness on their way to freedom. Now, the example of her work is reminding urban African Americans and other people of color that wilderness is part of their legacy; that the skills of gaining an orientation in the world, knowing how to feed, shelter, and protect yourself from danger, are skills needed in both urban and rural settings. The exercise has had a parallel in a reenactment by a student group led by Charles Blackson on a 420 mile Underground Railroad route from St. Louis to Oberlin in northern Ohio.

Kamau comments: "I've seen young people come home from this and say, 'Momma, I can do anything!' So it boosts self-esteem. I've seen adults return, recharged, to counter racism with new fervor. And I've seen people, especially Whites, who've said, 'Now I understand racism from the other side's view.' I see that as positive change."

The story of Harriet Tubman—and of wilderness as sanctuary—lives on through Kamau Sababu Kambui, the Wilder Forest staff, and the thousands of people they have taken through the Underground Railroad. Fortunately, there are also young people among the indigenous communities of the desert who wish to carry on their grandparents' stories, to sustain their people's relations with the plant and animal world.

Daniel Pablo, a high school student at Indian Oasis on the Tohono O'odham reservation, is one such youthful preserver of nature and culture. I have known Daniel since he was four, when I would visit his grandfather Delores Lewis, one of the most hard-working and knowledgeable farmers in the O'odham community. As Delores and I would walk to his floodwater-fed field in the desert over a decade ago, Daniel was already following in his grandfather's footsteps, literally and figuratively. When I kid Daniel about this now, he laughs and explains: "Wherever he went, I used to follow him around. They called me the Shadow. I thought I was following him to get out of my parents' way. Actually, what I was doing was learning how to plant seeds, how to take care of plants. This is how I learned."

In July of 1992, when the first gathering of traditional Native American farmers was convened in Gallup, New Mexico, Daniel took the honor of being the youngest farmer present. His grandfather Delores Lewis was also present, traveling beyond the Sonoran Desert for the first time in his life. After Delores gave a blessing in O'odham on behalf of all the farming families present, the farmers took turns explaining their relationship to the earth and their community. Daniel was among the last in the circle to explain how he came to farming:

"One time I was playing with my cousins. My cousins asked 'Where's Grandpa?'

" 'He's probably out in the field,' I said. 'Do you want to go see him?'

" 'Yeah, let's go see him.' So we went, and sure enough, he was sitting under a mesquite tree. He was getting his seeds together, getting ready to plant them.

"There were three of us. Next thing you know, Grandpa said, 'Line up. Line up!'

"He gave one of us a kids a hoe, one the seeds, and another the shovel. 'All right, start walking. Take two steps and dig a hole. Take two more steps, and dig a hole. And you follow him and put three seeds in the hole. The next hole, next hole. You go along with the shovel, and bury it up, bury it up!'

"So he put us all to work, and I thought it was fun. I guess my cousins didn't really take an interest in it. So they figured out they better not go to see Grandpa or he would put us to work.

"I used to think my Grandpa was a real brave guy. I still do! When the monsoons come to Arizona, there's lots of lightning with the storms. Sometimes when it rained, I would see my Grandpa with his metal shovel on his shoulder walking into the fields when it was still raining . . . and making lightning!

"He would go out there and direct the water, or fix one of his dams if it was broke. He taught me how to do that—how to irrigate, how to have water sit in one area and soak in. He taught me lots of different things about how to harvest and thresh various crops. . . .

"I didn't really plant for myself when I was *young*. But when I turned ten, my father gave me a little plot of my own. He went ahead and tilled the ground, really working at it. He got my cousins out there working on it with us for a long time. All day. The time finally came to bring in our harvest: corn, beans, squash, melon. I was pretty proud to see it, and my father was proud to see it.

"Two years ago, he passed away. I was isolated by myself for a while, and I didn't know when to plant—my father had always helped me, making sure that I planted at the right time. The ground had turned hard, so I didn't plant that first year, the year he passed away.

"The next year, I went out and started planting. I used my hoe and shovel to turn the ground over, and I put my seeds in the ground.

"About that time, a traditional dance group formed, the Cultural Exchange Youth Dance Group, set up by Save the Children

on our reservation. They asked me if I wanted to join, for they'd
be taking a trip to Philadelphia, Mississippi—as an exchange
with another Indian community—and they needed some dancers. I said, 'Sure, I'll go.'

"I had already told them that I would go along when I realized
that no one would be there to take care of my plants. My
younger brothers aren't really interested in the garden. I didn't
think my mother and grandparents would be able to watch over
my garden.

"So the time came for me to go. Where I live, the ground is
dry and everything is a dull brown color. But when I got over
there to Mississippi, I saw *all these trees*—always green and always
wet. I wished it could be like that at home.

"Then, one of our chaperons called home, and learned that it
was raining! It had started raining when we left, and it hadn't
stopped yet, two weeks later.

"When I got back home, it was dark, too dark to look around.
In the morning, I finally got to look around outside and saw
green all over! Hey, my wish came true!"

Daniel paused here for a moment, looking over at his grandparents, Delores and Margaret, who chuckled, then shifted their
glances downward, as if focused on the garden scene Daniel was
describing.

"Grasses covered the ground, the trees were all green! I ran
outside—around back to my garden—and looked. My corn was
big-tall corn! My squash was *really big*!" He doubled over, laughing uncontrollably. "The other thing that was really big was the
weed cover—*lots of weeds*.

"I was looking around, thinking it was good to be home. I
had thought that my garden wasn't going to come out very good
. . . but I was wrong.

"I guess my father—who had taught me how to do it—was
still watching over my garden. I never really said this to anybody

before . . ." His voice cracked, and he looked down at the floor, the earth, the same way his grandparents had done, "but I think that every time I go out to the garden, he's still watching over it."

Everyone in the room let the silence linger; a few wiped away tears. Daniel looked up again, finally: "I'm thankful for what he taught me, and I'm thankful that my grandfather is still here to teach me even more."

When I go out to the desert village of Big Fields, and see Daniel working with his rototiller, or helping his grandfather with the harvest of crops and wild foods, I feel relieved that the generations can still *regenerate* agriculture, culture, and story together. But to do so, they must work together at it, keeping the land in front of them and the background noise of television out of earshot. Ironically, it was during a filming of an O'odham garden for Phoenix television that such a connection between cause and effect first entered my consciousness.

I had been asked simply to introduce a Phoenix filming team to the famous O'odham educator, Laura Kerman, who has for years taught Indian, Anglo, and Mexican children about desert gardening and gathering traditions in school, park, and museum settings. Laura sometimes has difficulty hearing and getting around—she was in her late eighties by that time—so I decided to go along with the filming team in case Laura requested any assistance.

When it came time to turn the cameras on, a bouncy blonde news celebrity appeared out of the remote broadcasting van, wearing fresh make-up and looking for a picturesque setting in which to situate Laura, who had her gray hair tied back with a big ribbon, and a lovely old full-length skirt on. The newscaster instantly decided that they should not sit down, but should stroll around the garden which Laura and her brother have tended for decades.

"You'll have to hold onto my arm, then, and help me walk," Laura cautioned, "and make sure you say things loud enough for me to hear." The news celebrity shot a worried glance at the film crew, but as the two women began to walk arm and arm, Laura's teetering did not appear too awkward. The news director signaled for the cameras to roll.

"Well, Laura, you and the other elders out here on the reservation have made your living from the desert for a long time, gardening and gathering wild plants. . . . Tell me, why do you think the younger generation is not keeping up these traditions?"

Laura listened, stopped dead in her tracks, unloosened her arm, and pointed straight at the camera, frowning: "*It's that TV!* They're all watching *that TV!* They just sit around in front of it, they hardly go outside anymore, so how can they plow or plant or gather the fruit? That's the problem, *right there!*"

Her outstretched arm wavered as she pointed at the camera running in front of her. As the newscaster graciously laughed at the good joke played upon her and her television audience—the sequence was run, uncut and uncensored that same week—I noticed that Laura had not been the only one trembling. The man behind the camera itself was shaking. Whatever skill and habitual concentration he had brought to his work, the reminder that his viewfinder trains us to see so little of the world seemed to have shaken his confidence in what he was doing.

Neither the newscaster nor the cameraman are culprits so much as they are unwitting accomplices to a crime larger than that any TV news show could ever cover. It is a crime of deception—convincing people that their own visceral experience of the world hardly matters, and that predigested images hold more truth and power than the simplest, time-tried oral tradition. We need to return to learning about the land by being *on* the land, or better, by being *in* the thick of it. That is the best way we can stay in touch with the fates of its creatures, its indigenous cultures, its earthbound wisdom. That is the best way we can be in touch with ourselves.

G.P.N.

A Wilderness, with Cows

I

At sunrise, I tag along behind the three Dufurrena grandchildren, who walk behind their fathers, who, in turn, follow Buster, patriarch of this Basque sheep ranching family in northwestern Nevada. We move off into the sagebrush, looking for the herd, to check for newborn lambs that may need a little help from humans. I lag behind to photograph as the Dufurrenas disappear over a brush-covered knoll and emerge with the sheep in a draw below, moving toward the trucks. The rising sun flushes gold on the Jackson Mountains across the valley.

Later that morning, I follow Zackary (age eight) and Magen (age six) around the ranch, meeting Jim the calf, goats and ponies, a hutch of rabbits raised for meat, and Connie, the baby pig that Magen bought from the neighbors with all of her savings: $3.53. Zackary exults in drinking milk straight from the goats; his mother has socialized him just enough to squirt the stream into his mouth rather than suckle the goat directly.

The next day, when the time comes to brand spring calves at Texas Spring, a few miles from the ranch, Zakary, Magen, and their ten-year-old cousin Sam help their parents vaccinate, brand, dehorn, ear-notch, snip the chest skin to make an easy-to-recognize wattle, and, for steers, castrate the young animals. The kids line up on a board the sliced-off scrotums—puffs of soft fur in varying browns and blacks—to play with later. Magen has the job of carrying the freshly harvested testicles out of the corral to a waiting coffee-can. Most of these *cojones* are reserved for lunch back at the ranch; the rest of the delicacies, grilled on the propane-fired drum used to heat the branding irons, are savored by nearly everyone present. We stand in the haze of dust kicked up by struggling calves; my camera bags will emanate the characteristic smell of dust laced with the sharp reek of singed hair for weeks afterward.

The ranch life of the Dufurrenas lies on a continuum that runs from tribal knowledge of wild resources to life in the city. At each point along the continuum, the experience of growing up with the land changes; we pass further and further into a world isolated from other beings and from the land, into a world of strictly human concerns where we know nothing of our interdependencies.

Begin with tribal people. Hunters and gatherers depending primarily on nonagricultural resources and native farmers working in small fields in wild places learn a great deal about the nuances of seasonal cycles and specific life histories. Native people living in this way still exist, but increasingly they will live in cities, as does half the world's population today. Once a culture begins to move toward a wage economy, no longer directly in touch with food production, wild and agricultural resources are taken for granted. Children no longer absorb the details, make the connections, understand the whole.

Ranches and farms come next on the continuum. As anthropologist Joseph Jorgensen has noted, western American ranchers generally differ from farmers in their attitudes toward the land. Farmers consistently see their land as a possession with specula-

tive value. Typical western ranchers, says Jorgensen, value other
aspects of their lives more than the market value of their ranch.
They place at the top of their list: "vistas, open spaces, the
beauty of undulating grassy plains, predators, clean air, clean
and sufficient water, physical isolation of houses on the landscape, and disapproval of blatant trespass." Indeed, ranchers in
Montana, to their amazement, have found themselves in league
with Indian people in fighting mining and power conglomerates
intent on strip-mining grasslands.

Multigenerational families working directly with land, animals, and plants have become increasingly unusual in America.
Less than 2 percent of Americans now live in the country; one
out of four Americans who lived on the land in 1979 had moved
to town ten years later. Even in the West, three-fourths of the
region's people now live in cities, where the old romantic
imagery may survive without challenge: Marlboro Country,
tight-lipped cowboys and their good-hearted women, vanishing
but noble Indians, and wildlife either viciously predatory or doe-
eyed cute.

Though Indian people have plenty of other struggles, they do
have a guarantee of sovereignty over their land. Ranchers lack
even this stability, and their lifestyle—along with their grandchildren's chance to experience a ranching childhood—is endangered by the integrated national economy and urban values.
What will we lose if this way of growing up disappears? What
can such a childhood teach children about plants and animals
and land and family?

Though I am an urban westerner, with values many rural westerners would dismiss with snarling oaths about "envarmintal-
ists," I also believe that these ranch kids can understand their
home landscape in ways I cannot. They live closer to it; they
work with it; they depend upon it. For these reasons, we need to
pay attention to their lives before the chance to lead such a life is

gone. To learn more, I made several journeys from my home in Salt Lake City out into what writer Ivan Doig calls the "house of sky."

To travel to the Dufurrena sheep ranch is to journey into the country of space, into the far reaches of the Basin and Range. Such country greatly complicates the concept of "neighborhood." Isolated ranches and villages in the West generally depend on school activities—and constant, considerable driving—to create neighborhood. Basketball games and wrestling matches create a network of friendship and acquaintanceship over hundreds of miles. All the other connections that link people stretch across these same miles; and so, in this West, the Dufurrenas are my neighbors.

I began on the interstate, driving for 350 miles across the desert from Salt Lake City to Winnemucca, Nevada. There I turned off the freeway and headed into the empty country to the north toward a little town called Paradise Valley, where I veered off again toward Oregon, on the road to Denio—a town of thirty-five people reputed to be more isolated from a railhead than any post office in the country.

The basins here are remnants of Pleistocene Lake Lahontan—broad, flat, still, dotted with shadscale that lets the earth show between plants, a geologic place. As the mountains rise from these lowlands, sagebrush replaces shadscale. The day I arrive at the Dufurrenas, the violet and lavender and dun mountains lie under a low drapery of clouds from a mild weeklong April westerly. The Santa Rosa Range recedes behind me to the east. The Jackson Mountains loom south of the Dufurrena ranch, snow halfway down the slopes of King Lear Peak. Beyond, through the hint of a rain curtain, the Pine Forest Range rolls across the

northern horizon. Along a nearly thirty-mile straightaway
through this sea of desert with its island mountains, a little
wooden roadside sign seventy-five miles northwest of Winnemucca marks my destination: "Photo Gallery."

Linda and Buster Dufurrena live here, with their grown sons
Hank and Tim and their families. Putting up alfalfa may be 80
percent of their job, but they choose to call themselves ranchers.
They run 1,400 sheep and 400 cattle on the surrounding range.
Two herders from Mexico live with the Dufurrena herd along
Bilk Creek in the hills across the road from the ranch. Hank or
Tim or Buster checks with them mornings, bringing back to the
barn any lambs that will need some human doctoring or mother-
ing. In the evenings, one of the Dufurrenas tows the herders'
kitchen and sleeping wagon to wherever the sheep will bed down
for the night.

Linda is a photographer, and the gallery sign announces her
studio and exhibition space attached to the old ranch house. The
gallery doubles as the guest room, and I sleep here beneath
framed photos of shecpherders, children with lambs, and rural
Nevada landscapes. Hank's wife, Ginny, grew up in ranching
country across the Oregon border and spends her time working
on the ranch, bottle-feeding orphan lambs along with raising
Zackary and Magen. Tim's wife, Carolyn, came to Nevada as an
Ivy League–educated research geologist. She met Tim, stayed,
and they have a son, Sam.

Carolyn teaches in the Denio School (two teachers, thirteen
students). Male friends contemplating quitting their careers in
medicine or architecture ask Tim and Carolyn if a couple can
really make it running a farm or ranch. Carolyn says, "Sure, as
long as your wife has a teaching certificate!"

On weekends, three generations of Dufurrenas leave before
dawn to check the night's crop of lambs. After the morning out-
ing, all return to the ranch for breakfast. Later in the day, Zack

and Magen visit with Tim and Hank and Buster each time the men come back between chores for coffee in the main house—the grandparents' house. These children come close to an ideal of self-sufficient living close to the land, resolving the tension between culture and nature by integrating work, home, and family. What do they learn from even an approximation of this ideal? Is this dying lifestyle worth saving?

The children of Ruby Valley, Nevada, also live in a home dominated more by landscape and animals than by people. A three-room school (grades one through eight) serves some forty children who live up to sixty miles away. The valley has no town. The children live on ranches that lie at the mouths of canyons draining the east face of the Ruby Mountains, the lushest and most Sierran of Great Basin ranges.

Home for Ruby Valley children begins in their yards, with a tree to climb, and extends into their fields, bordered by willow thickets to hide in, and with plenty of open space for riding horses and raising 4-H livestock. The day I arrived at the school, everyone wanted to tell me about Henry Krenka's cattle drive passing through the night before, with six-year-old twins riding the full sixty miles down the valley for the first time. Home also reaches up the neighboring creek and right into the mountains. The children picnic and fish in the mountain creeks, and they revel in these secret places and take pride in their knowledge of them. I learned from the children, not their parents, which canyon to return to on a camping trip with my family.

Isolation brings with it both gifts and complications. Wanda, the school bus driver, mapped out for me the route of the 105-mile daily bus run. No store exists in the valley. Everyone must go to town to shop and must move there to attend high school, and so the children's world automatically includes Elko, seventy miles away. One 1993 guide to the good life proclaimed this growing city with a community college and twenty thousand people the "best" small town in America: "where the traditional values of family, community, faith, hard work and patriotism remain strong." The world of Ruby Valley children also may include visits to Salt Lake City, four hours away, the most accessible urban area. What seems an isolated life thus has significant connections to wider horizons.

In Ruby Valley, children continue to have powerful and direct experiences with animals, though mostly with creatures bred for human purposes (a fact of ranch life made clear in my time with the Dufurrena kids). Ruby Valley children hunt jackrabbits, routinely see deer, raise pigs and lambs from birth, herd cows, cut hay, worry about the dangers to their family's stock posed by coyotes. They learn early about mating and breeding behavior, and routinely see births and deaths, assisting with both.

As they grow older, values change. Younger Ruby Valley students (grades 1–3) told me that their favorite plants were flowers, apple trees, sagebrush ("because you could make forts out of it"), and grass ("because you can hide from your brother in it"). Girls, especially, loved lilacs, roses, and tulips. Westerners may feel comfortable with space and aridity, but the silky lushness of rose petals and heady scent of a lilac bush heavy with blossoms remain irresistible—and dramatic in their contrast to the western environment.

By the time the kids reach sixth grade, however, they begin to sound more like their parents; they mention alfalfa as a favorite plant, "because I make money cutting it." Nearly half the older children chose cows as their favorite animal because cattle, too, turn a profit. Only one student spoke of a nonnative animal (the cobra) known only from books or television nature shows as a favorite creature. Other students mentioned rattlesnakes (because they are good eating) and antelope (because there aren't very many of them nearby). In this desert, children fix on the aspen of their mountains as a favorite plant because the trees give shade. When I asked them what would make the valley more perfect, there was a chorus of voices: "More water."

Few valley children, however, will ranch here as adults. Rod McQueary, a Ruby Valley rancher and cowboy poet in his forties, says: "There are only so many ranches, and they can only support a given number of people. Of the seventeen males who were ranch kids in my high school class, only two of us now live on ranches."

Ruby Valley remains McQueary's home. He told me: "I want to teach my kids traditional skills—riding, roping, horsemanship. They need enough of the basic traditional mentality to know where they're from and who they are, for a sense of self-worth. And they need a good enough education for a resume. Between those two things, they can do anything. If you only have one, you have no choice."

Twin Bridges, Montana, is a major step away from the isolation of Ruby Valley, one step closer to the lives of farmers and village folk. Twin Bridges, with about 450 people, provides services for the surrounding ranch country. About half the students in the elementary school live on outlying ranches, the rest in town. Dillon, with 4,000 people, a variety of agricultural dealerships and services, and a community college, lies less than thirty miles away to the south; Butte (ten times larger than Dillon), only forty miles to the north.

Here in southwest Montana below the high ranges of the Continental Divide, the ranches lie near the river bottoms, well out from the mountains. Fields take precedence over wilder country in the awareness of children. This struck me as a sharp contrast to Ruby Valley, where the ranches hug the base of the range. Twin Bridges fifth-graders told me of eating their favorite plant, peas, while driving the family combine; they like to suck on alfalfa and sweet clover, and they argue over the proper techniques for doing so.

The Twin Bridges kids, as a group, have moved one step away from immersion in the land; book-learning has become a powerful influence in creating their awareness of nature. And so, as favorite animals, along with their horses (because they are fun to ride), elk (because they are good to eat), gophers (because you can shoot their heads off), and cows (because you can work with them), they chose the new and exotic: nonnative pandas, jaguars, cheetahs, Siberian tigers, and snow leopards.

Paradoxically, this step away from daily contact with a wild landscape also gives Twin Bridges children a little of the fresh perspective of the outsider, the *visitor* to the mountains. With this step outward they bring to bear a new discriminatory attention, a sense of wonder. And so, when I asked them to name their favorite plants, several chose plants native to the mountains rising above their valley, plants not part of their daily routine: bluebells, arrowleaf balsamroot, shooting stars, and bitterroot.

If we have a need for connection with other beings, if what ecologist E. O. Wilson calls "biophilia" directs us toward the living world around us to fulfill part of our emotional needs, which animals, then, best suffice to meet those needs? Does working with cattle or raising pigs make us more or less sympathetic to endangered species? Does a ranch child feel more passion about maintaining a healthy range she rides through every day than a city kid who wants to save the rain forest but will never see it at all?

The children who gather each day in the village of Twin Bridges to attend school suggest that the answers to these questions are complex.

They live in between, with the experience of farming, ranching, and visits to surrounding mountains balanced by village life and an awareness of larger towns close by. Some children work with animals, and television tigers cannot match their own horses for vividness. For others, nature shows beamed into the family satellite dish from the blackness of space bring their most dramatic encounters with wildness, with other beings.

For both town kids and their cousins doing chores out on the ranches, a strong sense remains that Twin Bridges, Montana, has a unique place in the landscape. The town lies on the Jefferson River, near the confluence of the Beaverhead, Ruby, and Big Hole rivers. The Tobacco Root Mountains rise above these valleys. Children live here with a daily awareness of geography, unlike children in many more urban places. Flora, fauna, and land help to define their home, and in responding to my questions, they made clear that they understand this relationship.

▲　　▲　　▲　　▲　　▲　　▲　　▲　　▲　　▲

I I

Exactly half of the West is public land. Livestock graze 70 percent of the region. Outside its cities, the West is a wilderness, with cows.

All Americans own two-thirds of Utah; you and I own 85 percent of Nevada. Though the locals will never approve, each American has as much vested interest in logging the old growth forests of the Northwest, mining the Great Basin ranges, and grazing the Chihuahuan Desert as do the citizens of Forks, Washington; Carlin, Nevada; and Van Horn, Texas. Children in these places grow up using the resources owned and shared by all Americans.

What does this West have to offer children as a place to live—whether on ranches or in towns? What different values will they bring to managing its resources if they come from Ruby Valley, from Phoenix or Seattle, or as a vacationer from Indianapolis or Boston? And, as they mature, can the children of all of these places learn to talk with each other? Can they successfully compromise as the West moves toward limiting grazing, mining, and other extractive industries, as it surely will?

In Indianapolis and New England, for children, a trip to the country generally means going off to camp or visiting a summer home—a patch of private land at the beach or in the woods, surrounded by many other private enclaves. In deciduous woods, the land is intimate, broken into glades, bays, and copses.

In the West, a trip to the country leads away from the city in any direction, into the dry and empty spaces of the public domain, open for everyone to explore. Western spaces overwhelm, but along with triggering inward contemplation, this expanse of emptiness turns many outward, toward the land.

The late Wallace Stegner, the wise elder of western landscape and history, understood this paradox: ". . . there is something in that big country that tells an individual not only how small he is but also tells him *who* he is." As a child on the Saskatchewan prairie he watched his father struggle to be a farmer on land that would never yield a living to a farmer. And he played with and killed any animal not domesticated or protected. Stegner summed up his childhood as "an idyll counterweighted by death": "There are two things that growing up in the West, on a belated frontier, gave me: an acquaintance with the wild and wild creatures, and guilt for my part in their destruction."

A truth about rural families underlies Stegner's reminiscences. As historian Elliot West notes of frontier children, while their parents labored close to the house and in the fields, the children's chores took them into wilder country, "gathering, hunting, and herding." This was true for both girls and boys until adolescence, when the girls were—to their resentment—restricted, pulled into the houses to learn to be domestic. In childhood, however, both sexes "were naming the many parts of their surroundings; they were discovering what they could do." In this way, the new land became more the children's world than the parents', more their *home*.

As they grew up, these people of the West came to take the rightness of their values for granted. Rural westerners came to believe the land is theirs—public domain notwithstanding. Ranchers, and ranch children, however, no longer can hold attitudes in isolation. There are too few of them and too many children of the cities with different values. What both urban pilgrims and ranchers striding through fields in their irrigating boots insist upon, of course, is that their needs must be addressed fairly. Ranchers insist that cows—animals that can make us Big Macs and provide a living for a family—are just as important as other resources, as important as families out for a camping or backpacking trip, as important as goshawks and Mexican spotted owls and Douglas firs.

Stegner, better than anyone, understood that the future of the West depends on all of its citizens working together to invent new ways of living here. We will need the wisdom of locals, who know the land first-hand, and the wisdom of city people, who may see broader issues. Everyone must learn about the place and its dry facts of life. We learn this best in childhood—whether growing up on a ranch or visiting national parks and wildlands from a suburban home. The status quo must become dynamic, and the children of the West who know both sides will determine the flow toward the future.

In a 1992 survey of fifth and sixth graders in the United States, 9 percent of the children said that they learned environmental information from home; 31 percent reported that they learned from school; and a majority, 53 percent, listed the media as their primary teacher. Such media-inspired children may become fierce in their desire to save condors and whales. In Santa Fe, New Mexico, for example, each May, the children of as politically correct a group of yuppie parents as one is likely to find don the costumes of endangered animals for All Species Day and parade proudly through the downtown streets.

Contact with even common wild creatures has become rare for most American children. Central city children may have virtually no experience with native plants or animals. The most likely journey into wilder country for more affluent kids in northeastern cities takes them to summer camps. And so, a traditional boy's camp in Maine, Camp Timanous, stresses the development of "Mind, Body, Spirit" in a scheduled round of swimming, archery, ball games, sailing, and crafts. The local environment is mostly a playground for such activities, rather than a force in itself. According to the camp catalog, however, a focus on "nature and ecology . . . annually becomes the free-time favorite of a small group of boys whose interest leads them into swamps and woodlands in search of new wonders." The camp experience can be the catalyst that leads a child to look for such "wonders" in wilder and wilder places.

Ranchers and farmers, in contrast, earn their livings directly from other living things. Children in rural settings know viscer-

ally what many city children know only from television if they
know it at all: that milk and meat come from cows (indeed, din-
nertime steaks at a small ranch may come from a particular
bovine, named Vanessa or Pete), that plants grow our food in
seasonal cycles, that storms and droughts can destroy crops, and
that people can go hungry as a result. Farm and ranch families in
dry country relate everything to water; its abundance or rarity
pervades their lives.

A generation ago, Americans often had ties to relatives still living on the land. Families visited their country relatives on summer trips; these reunions were a routine part of people's lives.
Today, few urban residents have access to these connections. To
ride horses or be around cattle, "city slickers" must pay for a
dude ranch experience. If we value what can come from *living* a
rural childhood—from riding through cow pastures and playing
in sagebrush rather than on lawns, from tending horses rather
than hamsters—we must act to preserve the possibility of such a
life. It is disappearing fast, and those who are aware of its endan-
germent are fighting over the scraps and remnants.

Living in the West is hard work, with the roles of men and
women still defined uniquely, with plenty of work to go around.
When writer Jim Carrier asked Colorado rancher Polly Spann
about her husband's influence on their three daughters, she told
him: "They were honed with an ax. Lee told them: you have to
look like a girl, act like a lady, think like a man, and work like a
horse."

Writer Teresa Jordan, raised on a Wyoming ranch, emphasizes
what this kind of family-based learning does for ranch children:
"No one else in America has had the chance to learn, on such a
regular and broad basis, from their parents." She also notes that
both sexes must behave daily in ways that blur gender distinctions, working in a manner both strong and tender: "A woman
who pulls a calf in open country in sub-zero weather and then

wraps the calf up in her own coat to keep it alive knows something about fierceness. And a man who does the same knows something about nurture."

Working on the land gives children the age-old familiarity with animals most of us have lost. Ranch and farm kids rely on animals as friends where human friends are few and far between. Ranch women interviewed in Teresa Jordan's *Cowgirls* remember their childhood dogs and horses as their best friends: "I could talk to him, and he knew what I was talking about." The sense of separation that ranch children feel when lambs, heifer and steer calves, and full-grown pigs are sold for slaughter is powerful. And yet Jordan believes that "growing up ranch" teaches you about the basic rightness of this exchange: "You take good care of them; they take care of you."

Farmers must learn patience, the patience of waiting for crops to grow. A naturalist's immersion in wildness by observing birds, bugs, or mammals requires patience, too—a virtue learned through even a small dose of experience with the natural world. This direct experience teaches a patience starkly opposed to the unrealistic expectations fostered by television nature shows that must sandwich entire life histories between commercials. Such a parade of dramatic events does not happen often in nature. Children building forts, poking around ponds, climbing trees, and hiding in tall grass understand this.

Child psychiatrist Robert Coles was amazed by such patience when he spent time with Natalie, an eight-year-old Hopi Indian girl. He describes his reactions in *The Spiritual Life of Children*, after visiting with Natalie on her Arizona mesa, watching circling hawks, running with her dog, saying goodnight to her friends, the stars: "I started realizing how probing a naturalist she is (which is not unusual among Hopi children) and (more extraordinary) how preoccupied she could become: her mind seemed almost lost in thought, so engrossed was she with the land and sky, the sun, moon, and stars, the flowers her mother grew, the animals, the changes of light that came with clouds."

Ranch children learn in similar fashion about careful observation and nuance of behavior by taking care of horses and pets and stock. They also understand domesticated animals as utilitarian, existing to serve human needs. Death may move them, but it does not shock them. Their intimacy with animals is an intimacy with life. Teresa Jordan describes the end of a day during calving season: "We come in each evening splattered with mud and milk and manure, stained with blood and amniotic fluid, stinking of afterbirth. It's hard to convey the sheer satisfaction of it all."

Frontier American children worked prodigiously. However, the contribution of rural children to the actual work of production decreases with affluence. By the mid-twentieth century, working farm children in America did not pay their way until their late teens.

When I asked to photograph ranch kids doing their chores in Twin Bridges, Montana, I was taken to one of the less affluent operations in the valley, the Grose family's Open Cross Ranch. The mother, Jimilea, in her thirties, grew up on the spread. Today, she and her husband, Bill, run a ranch that depends for its survival on the contribution of their children. Randon and Krystyl Grose, eleven and nine, respectively, are proud of their contributions and, according to their teachers, they work harder on the ranch than they do at school. At bigger ranches, hired hands do the chores and the children spend their time raising pets or 4-H animals.

Jordan described to me how directly self-esteem was tied to physical competence for the children on her family's Wyoming ranch: the pride she took in what she knew, in being able to do a good job, in noticing things—especially, noticing something before an elder. "I learned how to read the landscape. I learned from watching animals. I didn't learn many of the names of grasses, but I did learn that if I was ever lost, I could follow any animal path and it would lead to water, that I could follow a fence and come to a road. I knew that you could eat cactus and that it had water. You could clip porcupine needles and they would come out easier from an animal."

Jordan also pointed out how ranch children shoulder responsibility early. At eight or nine, ranch children work alone. In round-ups, they are assigned a particular ridge; if they find no cows there, what do they do? How far off the ridge do they go? In looking at a distant field, they may see a cow lying down. Is it sick or just sleeping? Does it need doctoring? An animal may die if they do not make the right decision. Says Jordan, "If they live in a supportive family where the fact that they made a decision is applauded even when the outcome isn't perfect, they grow into decisive and confident adults."

At the beginning of the twentieth century, L. L. Nunn realized something was missing in American education. The leaders of society knew the classics but they no longer knew much about daily physical work and responsibility in the real world. In trying to balance these sources of learning, Nunn may have given us a model for teaching young people about the common ground that exists in the West between these opposing groups who distrust each other so much.

An industrialist and philanthropist, Nunn created Deep Springs College in 1917 on a 2,500-acre ranch in an isolated valley below the Inyo Mountains on the California and Nevada state line. Nunn's goals for the twenty-five male students—all on full scholarship, studying with a faculty of five to seven—still guide the two-year institution today.

In 1923, a year before his death, Nunn wrote of the Deep Springs experience of isolation, liberal arts education, and student management of the ranch and college: each student comes "not for conventional scholastic training; not for ranch life; not to become proficient in commercial or professional pursuits for personal gain. You come to prepare for a life of service." Nunn wished to train leaders, and he believed that the desert created them: "from Moses to Roosevelt . . . The desert speaks."

With a ranch manager and farmer as discreet supervisors, Deep Springs operates as a nearly self-sufficient community, with each student working at least twenty hours a week in every phase of ranch and school life, under a student labor commissioner—one of several rotating elective offices designed to promote learning by doing. In the words of former student and faculty member, now board member, L. Jackson Newell: "A breakfast table looks different to someone who has milked cows, churned butter, slaughtered hogs, candled eggs, and dug potatoes." After two years at Deep Springs, students transfer to Cornell, the University of California, Harvard, and the like.

Newell concludes: "Deep Springs alumni have (1) an awareness of the importance and dignity of physical labor, (2) an appreciation for wilderness and the solitude it affords, (3) a sense of the duty to invest their talents toward humane or public ends, (4) an awareness of society as a social organism dependent on the quality and good will of individuals, and (5) a lively cultural and intellectual life."

One way to measure the academic and social success of this approach: more than 60 percent of Deep Springs graduates hold doctorates or medical or law degrees. Those doctors and attorneys may not be environmental lawyers and rural general practitioners, but they carry with them the Deep Springs experience of wild desert, of western space, and of working closely with animals. In Jack Newell's 1982 study of alumni, nearly two-thirds rated the influence of Deep Springs on their lives as "very significant."

While holding to its values, Deep Springs gradually changes with the times. The ranch operation is now organic, avoiding pesticides and additives. The community continues to discuss the anomaly of its all-male student body, and may admit women soon.

A Deep Springs education clearly cannot be had by every child in the rural West. Ranch kids have the work experience but not the remarkable liberal arts classes. Most college students lack the chances for integrating real world consequences and labor with their scholarship. Jack Newell describes Deep Springs most pithily as a distinctive little "honors junior college." This does not diminish its ability to serve as a useful ideal. Life here melds wildness, work, and scholarship in a powerful way.

Remember, too, that similar experiences of only a few days can have profound effects. Rachel and Stephen Kaplan, in summing up their ten years of observations of participants in a Michigan backcountry outdoor education program note with excitement and surprise: "The experience with the environment changes us quickly and quietly. By and large it is not a process to which words are attached. Nor are people aware of how radically affected they are by the way they see the world."

Jennifer, a sixth grader at Twin Bridges, understands that wildness is a state of mind. She wrote this description of her favorite place outside: "I like it in the cow pasture because it is fun to run around and it does not smell like the city. It also is fun to watch the cows graze and the calves play. In the summer you can lay in the grass and stare at the sky. During a rain storm you can stand and watch the lightning. You feel like you're part of the storm."

The stereotype of wilderness as a pristine realm untouched by humans doesn't fit with the reality of wildlands cropped by native peoples for millennia in ways both subtle and dramatic. The complementary image of ranchers as universally rapacious destroyers of the landscape does not fit, either. Many families remaining on ranches in the West consist of people like the Dufurrenas who care about preserving their place and their way of life. Both rancher and vacationing backpacker value the land. Both want to protect open space. Both plan on being in the West for a long time.

And yet, rural economies are dying: young people leave ranches for cities to look for jobs, and the landscape can now be recognized as fragile and finite. Urban Westerners are beginning to think of surrounding wildlands as extensions of their homes, as shrines and ceremonial landscapes—crucial to use, but in ways that do not use them up. City families drive out into open country in their campers and compete for space with the families who have lived in the rural West for several generations. The weekenders would prefer to not see cows; the stockraisers grow tired of gates left open, trashed campsites, and what they see as general insensitivity to their contributions and knowledge. More and more, both groups together will need to work out a future for what is now *their* land.

Finding spiritual sustenance in the land requires a certain amount of solitude, but the experience clearly does not require a full-blown wilderness setting, nor does solitude need be absolute solitude. Natural history writer John Hay, for instance, spent a recent summer digging in his Maine garden, "waiting for revelations."

One urban friend described to me how she could stay connected to landscape in the row-house heart of San Francisco.

Jogging and walking the family dog, she can watch the earth turn toward spring as first crocuses and tulips bloom, next daffodils, then forsythia and lilacs. At dawn, crimson replaces violet in the eastern sky just before the sun breaks the horizon. Moments later the full moon sets behind a pale lavender curtain in the western sky. The sunrise triggers a chorus of birds as long as buildings offer a roosting place for starlings, house sparrows, and pigeons. Storms rip through the city, rain beats on roofs, fog lifts and settles. Sitting on her deck sipping coffee, she may look up from the Sunday paper to glimpse anything from the sudden stoop of a peregrine falcon to a migrating hummingbird in the backyard lemon tree.

Every childhood landscape comes with a different set of building blocks from which to construct a life. And that childhood experience—rural, village, suburban, or urban—lasts throughout life. In his memoir *Hole in the Sky*, William Kittredge wrote of his childhood in southeast Oregon ranch country many years after he had left home. He realized that Warner Valley, still, was "the main staging ground for my imagination."

In creating a stage for our children's stories, we make choices. We stake out the geographies of their childhoods in home landscapes, consciously or unconsciously. To do so attentively begins by thinking as a native of a region. We become part of a particular world of earth and plants and animals and humans.

For both rural and urban Westerners, such attention to wildness turns into rootedness only if the West is home. And "home" today must embrace more of the West than ever before. Ranches cannot exist unless they cooperate with cities. Urban people do not wish purposefully to obliterate rural people, though they can. At the least, cities are demanding reform from those who work with the Western landscape.

Rural children in the West learn about animals and aridity and work and patience. Urban children learn about worldwide envi-

ronmental problems, change, technological facility, the politics
of diverse populations. More and more overlap exists in what
each learns. Still, either may grow up to be suicidally stubborn in
their values.

The land can help steer them toward cooperation. Learning in
childhood the subtleties and secrets and limits of this arid public
domain called the West may allow us to have the understanding
we will need. The diversity of lives shaped by Ruby Valley and
Twin Bridges, Los Angeles and Denver, leads to diversity of
vision—and maybe, just maybe, the astonishing chance to pass
along to our children a healthy and distinct land and many com-
patible ways of living with its wildness.

S.T.

*L*aura Rose, then eight, was already out on the porch, peeking around to the sunny side of the stone cabin, when I came out into the canyon that morning. She craned her neck to watch something on the cobblestone wall.

"It's his land, Papa."

"What?" I yawned. "Who?" I stretched. "Whose land?"

She wriggled her little finger at me, one of those "Come quick!" signals. I too peeked around the corner of the cabin, and scanned the sunlit wall.

"It's *his* land, see?"

Basking on a cobble high up on the wall was a huge desert spiny lizard. His scales sparkled in the light as he rocked back and forth from the wall.

"Don't you think he's doing those push-ups to tell us it's his land?"

Meanwhile, Dusty was up at the Riggs Ranch corral, where earlier that morning his younger sister had been helping him noose fourteen lizards. Spinies. Whiptails. Collareds, Trees, and Zebra-Taileds. After having been lassoed with a tiny dental floss lariat dangling from the end of a stick, the lizards had been released inside a dry porcelain bathtub where they sat and sunned themselves atop cobbles and cross-sections of tree trunks the kids had provided. When Laura and I walked up the hill to see what had been captured, Dusty was sitting propped up against the bathtub, lizard in hand and field guide in lap, trying to identify one of the captives. The call was a tough one, we later realized, for although the lizard was a Zebra-tailed, it was about ready to molt off a layer of skin, and the diagnostic stripes on the tail were no longer sufficiently dark to guide us in our taxonomic exercise.

As I sat and helped the kids key out the lizards, then let them go, it came to me that I had had no such comparable experience as a child. My children were already more adept in the naturalist's skills of seeking out, securing, and studying lizards than I had been over the bulk of my biological career. There are gaps in anyone's formal education and backyard experience. In my case, one of the largest gaps squirms with snakes, lizards, turtles, frogs, toads, and salamanders. While my craving to know other organisms has led me to wetland birds and roadside gourds, wild mountain beans and marine peanut worms, desert bighorn and succulent century plants, I have somehow slipped over reptiles and amphibians. In my personal lexicon, these have all been lumped together as "herps." That's Greek, meaning "creeping things."

My own children's intense herpetological interest in catching, handling, and naming lizards still baffles me. Why are some children inclined to bond with animals that most people find unappealing, esoteric, or even frightening? Is this relationship in any way different from the more familiar link between children and common house pets such as dogs and cats?

In ruminating over these questions, I have been led back, searching for herps, into the dark recesses of my own childhood, to basements, puddles, and rusty sewer pipes that I had not revisited in more than twenty years. As E. O. Wilson has suggested, "The snake and the serpent, flesh-and-blood reptile and demonic dream-image, reveal the complexity of our relation to nature and the fascination and beauty inherent in all forms of nature. Even the deadliest and most repugnant creatures bring

the endowment of magic to the human mind." And so, I
returned to the Stomping Grounds of the Dinosaur, the Chasm
of the Snake, and the Lake of the Kamikaze Lizard. In a rather
painful way, I finally learned that this *is* "their land" as much as it
is other creatures', and that I had been ignoring that fact a good
part of my life.

Oddly, my earliest encounters with reptilian images remain
firmly lodged and vivid in my memory. Before I turned five, my
older brother Norman frequently took me down to the darkest,
most mildewed part of our basement to encounter "the underworld." Our home had been built into a sand dune not far from
Lake Michigan, and had thick concrete block walls that steadied
the house against the shifting and settling sands all around us.
My brother loved to go down into one particular dark corner of
the basement with a flashlight, where he would show me a chalk
drawing of a dinosaur that someone had once marked on the
wall. Because the sketch was tucked away behind some loose
paneling, it clearly predated our parents' tenancy, and therefore
had for us the veracity of a Paleolithic cave painting. We believed
that whoever had drawn it had actually seen a dinosaur nearby.

Not far from the dinosaur drawing was a hatch that allowed
hose access to an oil furnace; we always thought that it was a
crawl space running all the way beneath the house. Norman had
conjured a vision—derived from some frightening phrases my
parents had tossed his way to discourage him from exploring
behind the hatch door—of a primeval underworld. He shared it
with me in excrutiating detail.

According to his mental map, the crawl space did not stop at
the back wall of our home, but tunneled into the dune, and came
out beneath the small interdunal swamp just beyond our yard.

There, in the tunnel, he claimed, dinosaurs, crocodiles, and vampire bats still roamed in the dark. The picture on the basement wall verified either that someone had been down there once, and had escaped to record his or her sightings in chalk, or that, on rare occasions, these monsters would surface into the swamps and dunes surrounding us.

Whichever the case, Norman and I had plenty of fodder to fuel the fantastic bedtime stories we told to each other, and some left over for unanticipated episodes in nightmare form. It strikes me now that fear and awe of mythical lizards predated my knowing any in the flesh. Or at least, the occasional racerunner or skink that I could have seen while romping in the dunes had ballooned up to mythic proportions before my very eyes.

A similar phenomenon occurred with snakes. The most poignant memory of my boyhood happened on the last day of summer vacation, before I was to enter first grade and so begin a twenty-year sentence in academia. I took my shoes off after my last day of kindergarten and would hardly put them back on again until Labor Day. Between the Lake Michigan beach a few blocks away, and oak woodlands full of trails, there was plenty to keep me occupied outdoors all vacation long.

Early in the summer I happened on a female hiking companion, a quiet five-year-old from Pittsburgh whose father had transferred to the Gary, Indiana, steel mills to work a few months supervising a construction project. Our parents let us wander together in the woods behind our houses for hours on end. We walked hand in hand, seldom speaking, down the trails between forested dunes, and I would introduce my friend to all the local characters that she had not known in inner-city Pittsburgh: dragonflies, sassafras, prickly pear cactus, and jack pines.

We would stop along the trail, and one or the other of us would point to something that captured our attention, then name it: "Squirrel," she would say.

Or, "Strawberries," I might add.

"Raisins?" she might ask.

"No, maybe bunny poop."

After two months of such minimalist nature interpretation, I felt a closeness that I did not achieve with any other female until I was a teenager. What I remember most from that summer of being five was the very last day I spent together with my quiet friend. She was about to move back home again, and we were holding hands, leaving my house to walk back to the one her parents had rented for the summer. But there, on the front steps that dropped down off our little dune to the street below, we spotted a garter snake. Perhaps it was a Chicago garter with black bars across its lateral stripes of black and olive, one that discharges a sweet heavy musk and flattens its body when alarmed by children or other creatures. We gingerly stepped up onto the cinder block retaining wall above the stairway, and watched, eyes wide, as it crept up one after another of the dozen or so concrete stairs. It was larger and more lithe, magnetic and more malevolent, than anything we had ever seen in the flesh before.

Suddenly, I was hit by vertigo. I lost my balance, let go of the hand of my little friend, and fell, head-on, down the stairwell. I tumbled past the stairs where the snake had been ascending, and hit my head hard on the concrete, bursting blood vessels just above my eye.

I remember getting up, screaming, crawling up the cinder block railing to avoid the snake, and running to reach the house atop the dune, but I blacked out before I made it even half-way.

Following a brief trip around the corner to the family doctor's house, I sat with ice packs on my forehead for one whole day. I started school with one eye nearly swollen shut, my face bloated and bruised a pathetic color of shiny purple. The kids in first grade glanced at me, wincing, as if I were made up for Halloween two months early.

But that was not the hard part. I never saw my little girlfriend, nor the snake, ever again.

These early encounters with reptiles, real or otherwise, were purely emotive. They left their scars. But they are not unlike the typical confrontations between herps and most children who have had no chance to familiarize themselves with a variety of real reptiles. In fact, they are not much different from the experiences that adults have with all sorts of snakes and lizards. The "real" animals themselves remain largely unfamiliar, stripped of their life histories and ecological contexts, but pumped up full of mythos. The awe and fear of reptiles is seeded deeply in our evolutionary history.

If biologists Balaji Mundkur and E. O. Wilson are correct, most primates meet snakes with fear and loathing, for good reason. Snake bites have caused trauma, illness, and death to primates for millions of years, so that it is truly adaptive to take flight whenever slithering elongate forms come into sight. Wilson has recently written on how serpents came to loom so large in our collective subconcious: "constant exposure through evolutionary time to the malign influence of snakes [has led to] the repeated experience [becoming] encoded by natural selection as an hereditary aversion and fascination, which in turn is manifested in the dreams and stories of evolving cultures."

The mythical aspects of these animals get deflated somewhat by the facts and "safe sightings" of snakes that children begin to accumulate as they reach the age of ten, or thereabouts. According to Steve Kellert's wildlife attitude interviews with hundreds of children, youngsters between ten and thirteen shift their focus toward cognitive understanding of animals based both on personal and vicarious experience. Even at this age, however, most children do not learn much more about amphibians and reptiles, for they are considered small, ugly, scaley and slimy, unintelligent, dangerous, and too distant from humans in their history, behavior, and appearance. Snakes and lizards have achieved the status of being listed among Americans' ten least-liked animals, and are relegated to levels not much above those of cockroaches and mosquitoes. Most Americans simply do not empathize with reptiles in the ways that they do with charismatic mammals, or even with beautiful birds.

In my case, it took me a long time to grasp anything about the animals themselves, but I did learn fairly early on about how reptiles were vanishing from the world around me.

When I was between nine and twelve, a lizard came into my life briefly, then flashed back out again. It came at a time when I was getting to know the pecking order of all the boys within a quarter mile of my home. "If you have a model airplane you don't need," one of two mischievous brothers whispered to me at school, "bring it over, and we'll do something powerful to it."

I had two or three plastic models, and selected the best, a Blue Angel jet, to share with the gang that had newly accepted me into their fold. The next Saturday morning I walked a few blocks down to where I found my friends, all on their hands and knees, peeking into some storm sewer pipes stacked on the edge of a construction site.

"Put your model down and turn on the water faucet over there!"

"Yeah, bring that hose over here. We'll get 'im!"

"Get what?"

"The lizard, dummy! What else hides in pipes?"

I brought the running hose over to one of the older boys, who stood at the high side of the pipes. My schoolmate Joey signaled me over to his side, where he and Demetri were huddled.

"Which one is the lizard in?" I asked.

"We don't know, that's why we're gonna flood him out, spray the water in each one 'til we get him." They gave me two pipes to tend, and I peeked down their metal tunnels. I didn't see anything. I said so.

"Oh, come on!" Joey grimaced. "You don't have to *see* anything so long as you block the pipes when the water starts gushin', 'cuz the lizard will run against your hands."

I stood guard over my two pipes, a hand cupped over each opening just as Joey was doing next to me. The older guys began squirting the water; I could see Demetri getting antsy.

Suddenly, I felt something wriggle against my right hand. I moved the other hand over to better block off the opening, and pinned the lizard against the lip of the pipe with my right, just as the water began to trickle out. I grasped the lizard with both hands, and tucked him against my belly.

"Stop squirting! Gary got 'im! Get the string, the boat, and the cherry bomb!"

While I tenderly held the racerunner against my shirt, and looked at his legs and stripes and scales, the other guys ran around madly. Finally, Joey came back to get me and the lizard.

"Wait 'til you see. We're gonna tie him onto your plane and put them on an aircraft carrier out in that big puddle."

"Aircraft carrier?"

"It's just an old piece of wood we sawed down, but it floats real good out in the puddle."

Before I knew it, one of the older boys had tied my Blue Angel to the wooden launch, and plopped a cherry bomb in the open cockpit. Then he motioned for me.

"Bring the lizard over here. I got the string ready."

I surrendered the racerunner, but was still unsure what would happen next. Nick, who had obviously done this before, carefully wrapped the lizard against the Blue Angel fuselage, looping the string around both of them dozens of times.

"Let me tie it off now. Hey, gimme a knife so's I can cut the string. Hey, man, look at that! Lizard kamikaze pilot ready to go!"

"Where'd them matches go? Keep the boat upright or you'll get the fuse wet, dummy!"

By this time, nine or ten boys had assembled around the boat on the edge of the puddle. Then Nick turned to me.

"Hey, Gary Paul, you get over here. You brought the plane, you got the lizard, so you launch the boat. I'll light the fuse. Don't push it too hard or it'll flip! Hey, you little kids, get out of the way, or you might get blown up too!"

A queasy feeling came over me. I can't claim it was triggered solely by concern for the lizard, though I'm certain that for a moment I felt its life pulse within my grasp, and later regretted its death. Nor was it the loss of the model plane, since it wasn't that well made. It was more an anxious feeling caused by the costs of being part of a group of males on the loose. I was an accomplice to killing an animal, and destroying a piece of handi-work, all for the excitement of being part of the gang.

As the Blue Angel exploded, I closed my eyes, wanting not to see lizard flesh flying in every direction. The blast was still booming in my ears when I heard one of the other boys yell, "What can we do next?"

I decided to depart. I walked back home on a sandy trail, rather than taking the sidewalk where other kids might see me. From that time on, I've often had doubts about being in any group of humans out to entertain itself; it's easy for me to remember that the volatile mix of egos often leads to a sudden explosiveness that can degrade humans as well as other creatures around them.

I would not catch another lizard for many years.

Fortunately, not long after my loss of innocence at the Lake of the Kamikaze Lizard, I had a chance to aid rather than undermine a reptile in trouble. It was a chance encounter. My father and I were returning from a visit to some of the Nabhan clan who lived a few sand hills and swamps away, on land that today forms the ragged edge of the Indiana Dunes National Lakeshore. On the way home from his sister's home, my father decided to try a new inroad into an area recently opened to construction, and turned on to the paved entrance route into a planned residential development.

The land developer was later indicted when the walls of many of the houses he built atop backfilled wetlands began to sink and crack with the settling of sand into marshy mucks. But at the moment we entered his subdivision in the making, the surrounding community was giving this developer credit for showcasing fashionable, affordable homes, and for draining mosquito-infested wetlands. I was oblivious to any moral overburden associated with the scheme until my father stopped the car in the middle of the road. Startled, I looked up. My dad was looking out the rolled-down driver's window of the car.

"Son-of-a . . . I nearly hit a snapping turtle. Want to see it? You come on out your door, Gary Paul, but don't poke or paw at him."

I jumped out of the car. There, emigrating from a newly drained and bulldozed wetland, was the largest turtle I had ever seen. I had been exposed only to painted turtles before, and then usually at the funerals my friends had for these pets after they had forgotten for a few days to change or replenish the water in the aquarium. My father and I stood side by side as the snapper strode into the middle of the road, then stopped, bewildered by the headlight glow.

"It's lost its home. I'm afraid it'll get run over if we leave it here," my father grimly admitted. "Grab that pair of leather work gloves I have under the seat and give them to me. I'll put it in the trunk, and we can keep it in the bathtub until tomorrow morning when I can drop it off near a marsh away from paved roads."

As my father accomplished this task, I half-watched him pick up the turtle, now in the dark, and half-peered out where the headlights illuminated the surrounding woods and marshes. A bulldozer stood parked on a sand hill beyond a curve in the road, a hill like many I had walked over. The dune was being dozed down into the adjacent marshlands—sand, tree stumps, shrubs were being used as backfill for more house lots. I thought over my father's words, for I had never heard him express such concerns before.

"It's lost its *home*," I gasped. Suddenly, it occurred to me that humans would soon be living where animals once lived, and they would be calling that place *their* home. Even if the turtle had not been killed by our car, it had lost its habitat, as had countless other creatures we could hardly know, let alone rescue.

When we pulled up into our driveway, I wondered for the first time what our dune had been like before it had been built upon. Up in our bathroom, my mother filled the tub part way, my father's gloved hands brought in the snapper, and I offered a bowl of tuna salad on lettuce to our visitor. I sat on the throw rug on the floor, elbows leaning over the bathtub rim, and I watched the turtle until I could barely keep my eyes open. I wondered what it felt like to be homeless. Next morning, when I awoke, the bathtub was empty, for my father had already escorted our overnight guest out to some marshlands, so the two of them could get an early start on their work for the day.

I did not really learn much about that first turtle itself, except that the context of its life had been ripped up around it. For me, what had happened to the turtle posed a moral dilemma; I could not think of the snapper simply as an overnight playmate who came in his own shell. I began to feel that animals and plants deserved to have their homes protected, and I grew indignant whenever I saw habitat destruction around me: fewer ponds for turtles, fewer trails and play-hookey hideaways for me. I began to feel that turtles were important to have around, even though I might hardly ever see them, whether in the headlight glow, or through the field glasses, darkly.

And yet, the experience made me want to rescue other creatures, and to re-place them on safe ground. I became one of those "do-gooder environmentalists" at a relatively early age and soon took to salvaging plants and animals imperiled by the swath of the bulldozer blade. These gallant attempts at transplanting survivors never, however, imparted any lasting sense of satisfaction. Somehow along the way the loss of habitat became more disturbing to me than the loss of an individual organism. I realized that saving a single thread of life was different from saving the entire fabric through which that thread snaked its way.

I hardly had a chance to save "nature" as a whole, although as I grew older, I sensed more and more that my contact with it was truly saving me.

During the years between boyhood and manhood, an event would now and then erode at my herpetological fears. One year

Steve Trimble and I shared a cabin on a steamer out to several of the Galápagos Islands, and there we often set foot in places where we were instantly surrounded by marine and land iguana colonies, or by ancient tortoises too large and too full of character to ignore. One day during this voyage, one of our shipmates went off to sun herself and sleep on an abandoned beach. She was awakened by the weight of an iguana reclining on her torso; the lizard simply assumed that our friend would be a good perch upon which to sun *himself*! The woman was frightened for a moment, then quickly regained her cool; she simply rolled over to one side, dumping the lizard, then rolled back in the other direction to gain some distance. Hearing about this encounter was as close as I had come to imagining a relationship between lizards and humans.

Later I began to meet people who *did* have personal relationships with reptiles and amphibians, who actually paced their lives around the activities of lizards and frogs. Meeting ecologist Wade Sherbrooke was one such eye opener. He always had several species of horned lizards hanging around his place at any time. There, they would participate in ant-eating or camouflage experiments on his back porch, or he would incite them to squirt blood from their eyes (a horrifying strategy which these lizards have developed to scare away predators). I would sign on, now and then, to serve as a grunt worker for Wade's ground searches to find where different horned lizard species overlapped in range, and I became fascinated with the lore surrounding these armored, blood-squirting desert dwellers. I assisted other friends who would call me in the middle of a rainy night and invite me to count and sex spadefoots and Colorado River toads that streamed in to desert waterholes following the first flashflood of the summer season.

Yes, I finally had my hands on herps. By this time, I had learned to enjoy them, respect their ecological context, and consider the dignity of each individual animal, but I still did not share my friends' captivation with reptiles and amphibians. I was simply helping others in *their* studies, feeling no motivation of my own to go out and hug a herp each day.

It was not until Dusty and Laura caught lizard-looping fever that I ever really stopped to look the little guys in the eye and to catch the fever myself. Once the learning by doing became self-motivated *and* family-reinforced, I began to look for lizards everywhere, and to see them more for what they were. As I took on the heightened attentiveness of the lizard hunter, I came to notice a lot of other things about the world as well.

As with so many pleasures in my recent life, my wife Caroline served as the catalyst for this change. On one of our first camping trips together, Caroline taught Dusty, Laura, and me how to select supple sticks, how to tie slip knots at the end of the stick to make dental floss nooses, and how to approach unsuspecting lizards for the catch. I had seen this art practiced at a distance, but had never realized how subtle it was. You must dangle the noose close to the lizard's snout without casting a shadow across its eyes. You must also quietly capture its attention, so that when you flick your wrist to pull the noose over its neck, the lizard is caught off guard, and does not move out of the way of the descending lasso.

We all took to practicing this technique on whatever lizard we found lounging on the ground, or sunning itself against a stone wall. But while Caroline, Laura, and I shared similar ratios of hits and misses, Dusty excelled. *Excel* still does not tell the entire story. He became as captivated by lizards as they were by him.

Every few Saturdays, I would take Dusty with me to my office at the botanical garden, and he would quickly escape the indoors to disappear down the garden trails with his lizard stick. After I had sorted mail, cached some seeds, and locked up the office, I would go out to find him. Inevitably, I would come upon a crowd of tourists who had paused on their stroll through the garden in order to watch a little boy out on a rock, completely absorbed in stalking lizards. Whenever the noose dropped over a neck, and Dusty brought a dangling lizard into his hands to identify, the crowd would buzz and clap with delight, then disperse.

"It could be a *Urosaurus ornatus*, Papa, what do you think? Is it a male or a female?" We'd sit down with the field guide, flip the lizard over, stroke its belly to calm it down, then begin our inquiry in earnest. If Laura or Caroline were around as well, they too would help us in the holding, the assessment of sex, molting stage, and species, the discussion of behavior, and the delight in nature's designs.

What we were gaining was a sense of the other, a way of existence different from our own, different from what was already familiar to us. I don't know if such a sensibility can be formally taught; certainly lizard-looping can be, but what of the intimacy of passing a lizard hand to hand, through the family, each person recalling what other lizards it resembles, and where those brethren had been found? Lizards soon became part of our family story, indicators of where we had traveled, and how we had spent our time. If this sense of the other—and with it, a greater sense of belonging—can also be achieved through formal education, all the better for those who may not find it in their own nuclear family. But my guess is that such a sensibility is most richly transmitted through family and friends, where regard for lizards, in our case, is culturally reinforced over time.

All I am sure is that sooner or later, someone must simply take us by the hand, and show us another world. They must initiate us to the delight of encountering *the other* in the form of lizard, hawkmoth, or bat. They must move us out of our comfort zone and into the unknown terrain where lives somewhat different from our own still dwell.

My fascination with amphibians and reptiles allowed me to see that other individuals and cultures had been open to these creatures for far longer than my world had been. After years as an understudy to Native American elders who generously shared their knowledge of desert plants, I decided to try to learn from them about herps as well. One of them had, in fact, always referred to his childhood as the time "when I was out in the desert doing nothing but raising lizards."

At first I thought I would learn only the indigenous names for lizards, turtles, toads, and snakes. But it soon became clear that my friends knew much of the behavior, habitat, and food preferences of such desert critters, most of which I had seldom even noticed when I was out walking with these O'odham neighbors of mine.

Over a summer's time, I learned O'odham names and lore for nineteen different kinds of herps, and since then, their identities have slowly become better fixed in my mind. I had already known horny toads, desert tortoises, and Sonoran mud turtles, but now the characteristic traits and gaits of desert spinies, Western Whiptails, Zebra-taileds, and Side-blotched lizards came into focus. An O'odham elder, who once roamed with his family in semi-nomadic bands, told me that chuckwalla tails "tasted like chicken" and were deemed an oil-rich delicacy by her people. Other friends impressed upon me their particular respect for regal horned lizards, which if you tried to kill or bother them could bring on a psychosomatic illness the O'odham call "staying sickness."

"Even other animals have to be careful with those *cemamagi*," my old friend Delores said of the horned lizard. "I once saw that lizard caught in the throat of a dead rattlesnake, its spines poking up through the snakeskin. They know how to hunch their shoulders and make their spines stick out more when they get in trouble." It is not coincidental that Delores mentioned the hunching of shoulders, for horned lizards are said by other O'odham to cause hunchback.

My Pima Indian friend Culver Cassa went out with me to show pickled lizards to Chico Suni, the O'odham hermit of the Cabeza Prieta Wildlife Refuge and Bombing Range. Chico was not impressed by the smell of lizards in formaldehyde, nor by their lack of activity, for he knows each species by how it runs. Chico does a great imitation of a Zebra-tailed lizard running with its tail curled up like that of a scorpion.

Chico loved to roll the names of various lizards off his tongue. He rested on his back on an old cot while we showed him various lizards. He would glance at them, then let his hands dance in the air above him as he gestured their shapes and movements.

"That one?" he asked in O'odham. "Oh, that's *ko'oi tatal*."

"Rattlesnake's . . . uncle?" I asked, perplexed.

"*Tatal*—uncle on the mother's side."

"Oh, I see . . ." I said, amazed. He was applying the complex system of O'odham terms for kinship relationships to the affinities of various reptiles. In doing so, perhaps he was expressing his people's belief that there is just as much order in the relations between various animal species as there is in a human family or clan.

During these interviews, whenever Culver or I brought out certain lizards such as whiptails or spinies, the women would glance at them, then make themselves scarce. Culver and other friends gently let me know that there was considerable gender-related lore about these lizards, not generally discussed in mixed company.

Culver later conceded to explain the dilemma to Caroline and me over dinner. "I think that it's the one you call Western Whiptail. Some Pima think that if it goes into a young woman's house, she has to marry it."

"That must really make all the girls afraid of lizards!" Caroline commented. "If I heard a story like that when I was young, I would be so scared of lizards that I would never learn anything about any of them!"

Culver thought that comment over for a moment, then responded, "Oh, I don't know, I think our girls probably learn pretty quickly how to tell one kind of lizard from another *because* they have to worry about those Whiptails. It's not just any lizard they're scared of marrying, it's only that kind, and they get so they can tell it from the others pretty well."

Learning what to fear, and what not to fear, is a large part of growing up. My own slow coming of age regarding herps has been a gradual shedding of fears. Looking back, I can recall a dream which seems now in retrospect to mark a place where my relations with reptiles shifted.

During my last months living in the Indiana Dunes, I dreamt about the underworld reptiles that my brother and I had feared as children. The dream was triggered by another, then current fear. On the edge of the National Lakeshore, the NIPSCO electric company had announced its plans to build a nuclear power plant. Outraged, a number of my local friends had begun to work hard to stop its construction. Several of them kept me up late one night talking about the potential for thermal pollution of the adjacent bogs and marshes where early ecological succession studies had been done. We worried about the possibility of a nuclear accident.

I went to bed anxious, and despondent that the fate of the dunes seemed beyond our control. That night I dreamt that the nuclear power plant had been completed and that, during its very first run, a meltdown occurred. The radioactivity and "heat" from the accident destroyed everything immediately surrounding the generating plant and caused profound changes in the dunes where we lived. The local climate shifted, and suddenly, dinosaurs that had been dormant since the Cretaceous came out of hibernation. They emerged from the hatch in the basement of our old house.

The dinosaurs in my dream were terrifying in their fury, and their destructive rampage along the shores of Lake Michigan far exceeded anything I'd seen in the monster movies of the fifties. These demons tore up our streets and schools and stomped in the roofs of my neighbors' houses, squashing anyone left inside. They roared in rage and tore out the ornamental trees and plants in our yards and parks. Forced to return and live in the outer world again, they were clearing the scene of all human disturbance, making it habitable once more for themselves.

I'd heard the dinosaurs thundering toward the hatch door and had fled the house ahead of them, escaping to one of my old hideaways in the dunes. From a refuge there overlooking the town, I watched as they leveled my old neighborhood and dragged away the debris.

I wondered if I was the only one who had escaped and began to grieve for my family and friends, for the loss of my neighbors. Soon I began to cry aloud, not just for their deaths, but for the stupidity that had caused the nuclear accident and the reemergence of these monstrous reptiles. My weeping must have captured a dinosaur's attention, for when I raised my head, it had turned toward me.

"It's not that bad," the dinosaur finally said. "It's not as though your *whole* neighborhood is destroyed. The dunes and marshes are still here. And *we're* your neighbors now."

Scientists now claim that the part of our brain from which our most primitive behavior—our instinctive urges and reflexes— emanates is the part that is a holdover from our reptilian ancestors, one embedded deeply within the lobes of our more recently evolved mammalian mind. Freud guessed that such primitive behavior in us is purely sexual—that it is in place to drive reproduction and the continued fitness of the species. But I believe he was wrong; it is more than that.

The lizardness within us is our wild side. It is the ancient animal which some of us care not to acknowledge as part of our being. Because we put ourselves on pedestals above the rest of the animal world, we find it hard to acknowledge our affinity to lizards and snakes. They are not, we insist, as civilized, as sophisticated, as rational as we consider ourselves to be. People who flee for comfort zones in the presence of snakes and lizards are often the same ones who respond to their own vestigal behaviors with fear, distrust, or shame.

When we don't grow up meeting lizards, snakes, and frogs, we have no way to recognize their vitality and dignity, nor the continuity between them and us. We do not acknowledge them as our true neighbors. Yet, if we simply try to sweep them under the rug—out of sight, out of mind—they will rear up out of nowhere. Suddenly, they will surprise, frighten, or sting those who believe that their own reptilian sensibilities are fully extinct.

Better to seek out such reptiles, to make peace with them, to accept our old and complicated relations with them and accommodate them in our world order.

My hope is that my children's coming of age with the "crawling things" will be different from my own. I hope that their interest in and affection for reptiles will grow steadily from a foundation built on curiosity and trust. In coming to know the spinies and whiptails, salamanders and snakes, early and face to face, I believe Dusty and Laura will gain a lasting sense of respect for these creatures, and finally a sense of kinship with them. Instead of feeling mere dread, they will greet "the other" with the whole range of emotions and intelligent responses which any new encounter generates in those willing to learn.

G.P.N.

▲　　▲　　▲　　▲　　▲　　▲　　▲　　▲　　▲

I

*A*t twenty-six, I married a woman, adopted a dog, and, with the risks of responsibility, began to lose my innocence. I may have ceased being a child, but I had not yet reached adulthood.

The marriage was brief, but the dog lived with me for more than eleven years. As my companion in the wilds, he taught me how to share my life. Before fathering a child, I was father to a dog—and it helped.

We first saw him on the concrete floor of a cubicle at the Tucson Humane Society, waiting with equanimity for someone to rescue him—his nose resting between his paws, his brown eyes watchful under furrowed brows. He was two, and had been left behind by a military family assigned overseas. The card on his cage said: "Name: Jack. Breed: wolf/shepherd." I always believed the shepherd was Australian shepherd but never knew for sure about the wolf. One-syllable Anglo-Saxon "Jack" did not seem to suit this gentle, intelligent being. Since we lived in the Hispanic Southwest, we named him Carlos.

Carlos stayed with me when the marriage ended, since my life of fieldwork and writing suited his needs. At home, Carlos slept on the floor under my desk by day and, at night, next to my bed. Camping, he had the luxury of nestling close to my sleeping bag. Carlos learned to be a photographer's dog, curling up by my camera bag or digging himself a cool patch of fresh dirt to lie on while he waited for me to exhaust my ideas with a photo subject.

Carlos was good company. I teased him and talked to him—when I needed to talk but might have felt too self-conscious to talk to myself. I could amble along, watching for the small events that would become journal notes, and Carlos would not distract me from my reveries. He added another's life to my experience and connected me to the wild world in a way only a nonhuman life can.

I came close to taking him for granted. Twice, when I forgot he was out of the truck and drove off without him, I realized how much I would miss him if he were gone.

The first time, I had pulled over to sleep for a couple of hours one moonlit night near the mouth of Tsegi Canyon on the Navajo Indian Reservation in Arizona. I let Carlos out to empty his bladder, went to sleep, and woke up to a few spitting snow-flakes. Nervous about traveling in the storm, I cranked the truck to life and drove off.

Some fifty miles later, in the middle of Monument Valley, I addressed something to the back of the truck, and realized no one was listening (you could sense Carlos listening even when he didn't answer). Frantic—picturing Carlos dead on the high-way—I spun around, raced back, got a speeding ticket in Kayenta, and at 2:00 A.M. reached a spot near where I had left him. I began to stop every quarter mile and call into the darkness. Many Navajo dogs answered me from their owners's hogans. Finally, Carlos came trotting out of the night, back from his adventures, grinning.

The second time, I had been talking with Hualapai Indian people one summer evening, telling Coyote stories—or rather, talking around the edges of Coyote stories, since, in summer, one avoids telling stories that arouse the ire of what one Hualapai elder carefully referred to as "crawling long things." These were stories not just of any coyote, but of Coyote, the trickster-hero of Native America.

I left George Rocha's house in Peach Springs, Arizona, and drove a set of branching dirt roads headed for Madwita Canyon overlook, above the sacred place where the Hualapai lived with their gods in the Grand Canyon before emerging into this world. I stopped at a junction to hop out and peer at a fading sign, returned to the truck, and took the dimmer of the two forks. A few minutes later, a coyote (or was it Coyote himself?) trotted across the track through my headlight beams.

Some miles later, I reached the overlook, stepped out, and called Carlos. He was not there, and I realized he had jumped out when I checked the sign. I sensed Coyote laughing at me from somewhere off in the piñons. I drove back to find Carlos panting along the road trying to catch up, reminding me to pay more attention to him, to animals, to life.

Carlos's best time came in the early 1980s, when I spent months hiking with him in the Great Basin Desert, researching a book. Few human companions joined me on these trips. When I think of the Great Basin, I do not think of being alone, though some observers would say that I was. I think of being there with Carlos.

Carlos and I climbed peaks in isolated Nevada and Utah mountain ranges and walked frosted sand dunes on winter mornings. He curled into the roots of a four-thousand-year-old bristlecone pine while I photographed its branches. I watched him sniff at the view—as I looked at it—when we stopped at the end of a long switchback climbing into the Jarbidge Wilderness.

Carlos was known to chase squirrels, bark at deer, and keep pikas and marmots at a distance. He also provided counterpoint to my solitary perspective. His concreteness, his vitality, his simple affection, made the abstractions of the universe less ponderous. When I lay down in my sleeping bag on the enormous expanse of cracked mud polygons that forms the level floor of the Black Rock Desert playa and looked into a bowl of sky filled with stars, his warm back pushed against mine and his paws trembling in dreams of chasing jackrabbits helped me to comprehend my relationship with the Milky Way. He was another life, in a land so vast that I needed such grounding.

Tumult in other parts of my life seemed very far away at these times. Now, when I read the ramblings in my journals, the miles of walking come back, vivid. Sunsets watched between sips of scotch from an enameled metal cup flare again. Though each way of traveling in a landscape has its advantages, remembering the places I shared with this dog always cheers me.

11

When I was thirty-six, I married again. This one will last. My wife came West after college and swore ever after she actually had been born a westerner in the wrong place. As we walk and run rivers and camp together in these great spaces, another way of relating to the land becomes real for me.

My wife, Joanne, both enhances and distracts from what I see in nature alone. She asks questions and enthuses; we talk. In striving to articulate what we feel, how each of us reacts to the land, we use language earlier than I would alone to recreate the feel of light on sandstone or the smell of cliffrose. In some ways, I use up the words by sharing the experience; alone, I hoard them, secreting them away in my journal. Talking with the woman I love about the places we pass through makes the experiences warmer, simpler. The landscape becomes a part of everyday life, and I have trouble separating from it sufficiently to describe it as a writer.

At the same time, Joanne sees what I do not. She points out details I would miss. She questions things I take for granted; interested though untrained in natural history, she asks about birds and behavior and ecological patterns in an observant way that demands clarity and understanding in order to answer. She makes me think beyond where I might have stopped.

On the Black Rock Desert, we once took turns leaving each other. One of us would step out of the vehicle with no gear—no pack, no camera, no water bottle—and simply stand there in T-shirt, shorts, and thongs, with the silence ringing in our ears, while the other drove out of sight. Each of us had a few minutes alone, turning in circles, trying to orient ourselves in the endless miles of barren clay—a near-impossible task. The disorientation was stunning; it was delightful.

When Joanne drove back, the distinction between aloneness and sharing overwhelmed me. The difference was palpable, although both can bring joy.

By 1988, we had a daughter. When we began to hike with Dory, she rode in my backpack with her gurgles and small, singing sounds of wonder a few inches from my ears. She tugged at my hat, grabbed for my glasses, trickled graham cracker crumbs into the neck of my shirt, and craned her head to look around when I stopped.

With Dory, I forged yet another relationship with the land. I walked up mountains, and she slept on my back. I carried through the landscape the feeling of *family* that other generations of parents carried while migrating into North America along the ice sheets, or crossing savanna in Africa, looking for new country.

Parenthood demands everything I have to keep up with its challenges. Hiking with my daughter on my back gave me a sense of fragility and mortality I never had in the days when I always hiked alone. I walked more carefully, both when I carried her and when by myself, for there suddenly was so much to lose to a misstep. I felt vulnerable in a new way.

My sense of time changed forever when Dory was born. People on the trail asked, "How old is she?" Up to about ten weeks, I changed my answer every few days. After the answer could be calculated in months, I could let two weeks go by without marking the passage. But, oh, how different the passage of these weeks and months felt with this living clock in our lives. Wilderness time—the kind that slows when you hike for several days, the past and the future fading, until you live exclusively in the present—will never slow quite as much again.

Her birth transformed my parents and Joanne's mother from parents to grandparents in the moment she slipped from Joanne into my hands. Our only surviving grandparent, Joanne's Grandma Rose, died just four months after Dory's birth. The generations all bumped up a notch. We all moved a little closer toward death.

When Dory was about six months old—and I was more aware of life and death than ever before—Carlos began to fail. Organ after organ slowed until his liver gave out, and he stopped eating. I talked with the vet, who gave him only a couple of days on his own. Carlos maintained his dignity throughout his life, and I felt he should die with dignity. I made an appointment; the vet's secretary entered in her book, "Carlos: euthanasia." I took Carlos home for one last night curled at the foot of our bed.

The next morning, I looked into the brown eyes of my dog, said goodbye, and carried him in from the truck to the vet, to his death. He was weak and old, barely able to walk out the back door that morning to turn the snow yellow one last time. As rickety as he was, in my arms he still felt like Carlos, still my familiar friend of so many years.

The doctor injected him with the jolt of barbiturates that relaxed him so fast neither Carlos nor I had much time to think about it. One moment he lay on the table, alive. The next moment he sprawled on the table, dead. We wrapped him in a green plastic garbage bag, and I carried him back out to my truck. He felt warm and limp inside the plastic. He was not the same dog; I understood the meaning of dead weight.

I sobbed as I began the drive out to the desert to find a place to bury him. I was taking him to the Great Basin, the place where we had shared those fine days of solitude. It was the only place I considered. I would not mind being taken out there myself some faraway day.

I drove seventy miles. On the tape deck I played the first Bach cello suite and the choral finale to Beethoven's Ninth Symphony, music that suited Carlos—the first deceptively simple, the second intense but joyful. As I climbed between the Stansbury and Onaqui mountains, I pulled into a turnout near a line of hills overlooking Rush Valley, its sloping basin full of rough, aromatic sagebrush. The East Tintic Mountains, another small grey-blue range, rolled along the southeastern horizon under a high overcast. A front was headed in from the Pacific. I curled Carlos in his garbage bag into the main compartment of my backpack, shouldered it, and walked off into the piñon and juniper trees through calf-deep snow.

Carlos inside my pack? What an odd thought. I climbed a ridge, using my shovel as a walking stick, found an anonymous clearing between the little conifers, lay the royal blue pack on the white snow, and began digging a hole. The soil was rocky, full of cobbles eroded from the mountains in winter, washed down in summer flash floods to skirt the Stansburys with alluvium. I moved rocks, cut through roots, but did not dig deep.

At the bottom of the hole I put a small photo of Carlos with me and our old truck, a Zuni bear fetish carved with a heartline, and a chocolate chip cookie from a batch my mother had sent at Christmas—Carlos's favorite treat. Then I opened the pack and poured Carlos in a limp curl from his garbage bag. He was still warm. I tucked his teeth under his lips and moved his paws to a comfortable position. I stood back from the grave and leaned on the shovel.

I looked up at the horizon. I had done my crying. Carlos had a good life. This was the end of a time in my own life that had included more time alone, more time shared just with my dog, than I ever would have again. Family had ended my solitude; Dory was growing; time was ticking away.

I covered Carlos with stones, then shoveled earth back over his grave. It was deep enough to cover him but not deep enough to keep Coyote away.

My pack felt unnaturally light when I walked back to the truck. I was drained. I drove home. Joanne was out of town. I picked Dory up from the babysitter; I could feel my life ceaselessly pushing ahead, curving into the future.

That night, the front blew through northern Utah, softening the mountains, the silent basins, and Carlos's grave with a foot of fresh snow. I awoke the next morning to a sky scoured by the storm, crisp with cold, clean and crystalline, blazing with restorative sunlight.

Many weekends during the summer after Carlos died, Joanne

and Dory and I hiked in the Wasatch Range above our home in Salt Lake City. When fall came, closing in on the equinox, I could feel the seasons turn, the earth spin, time wheel by. On a day of special radiance, I walked down from a glacial basin through aspen forest, warm sun, cool air. Joanne was ahead, with friends. I walked along aware of the absence of my dog trotting beside me, occasionally pushing against my legs in affectionate reassurance. I was alone—except for a small, banana-smeared hand on my shoulder giving me a pat. And a coo in my ear, singing me down the mountain.

III

Jacob was born in 1991. Dory, like any strong-willed three-year-old displaced by her new brother from her father's backpack, ceased singing me down the mountain and took to whining me up the trail.

The birth of our second child changed the dynamics of our household. With our daughter, we remained two adults—with a child. Once we had two children, we truly became a family. That fact has enormous consequences on both our lives together and on the contrasting experiences with nature of our first and secondborn.

For three years, Joanne and I planned our family travels primarily to meet our own needs, keeping Dory in mind. On our journeys, however, Dory received the undivided attention that an only, or oldest, child enjoys. When we walked in the desert or the woods, I looked for burrows and beetles, leaves and feathers to point out. Soon she began to notice these things herself, showing them to me, noticing what I had not. Dory became my guide, if I slowed enough to listen.

For Joanne and me, camping had always seemed an athletic experience, involving hiking and climbing and the exultation of ending a day with a satisfying sense of tiredness, having used one's body efficiently to *walk* through the landscape. Good food and going to bed under the stars ended the day, our senses filled to the brim in the best way. With one child, our activity level remained high, for Dory simply came along in the backpack. With the addition of Jacob, even our non–goal-oriented hiking ground to a dead halt.

Now our family lives—and camps—in an intertwining flux of four personalities. Going to the land as a family is a social experience. We all sleep in the family tent. The two children interact with each other. Jacob's need for an afternoon nap meshes with Dory's need to explore around camp and to have our undivided attention for a reasonable interval; we stay put. I trade my solitary intimacy with the earth for the chance to share in my children's small discoveries. Doing what we must to end each day with everyone happy in our temporary home replaces seeing miles of new country as the measure of a successful trip.

Parent and child mutually reinforce each other's enthusiasms, right from the beginning. As a newborn, Jacob calmed down whenever we took him outside in his carriage. When he is fussy at a year-and-a-half, I still take him for walks. Another couple's newborn girl quieted when carried out to watch the evergreen trees waving against the sky at the family's cabin in the Wyoming woods. Babies and parents are learning and teaching: the outside—"nature"—is a soothing place of refuge, filled with interesting things.

As the months progress, infants make more sophisticated choices, fixing on their favorite objects. Jacob looks for birds at the backyard feeder the first thing each morning and the last thing each night. When he was fifteen months old, I joined Jacob and Joanne at a window, and he enthusiastically pronounced his first sentence: "Daa—birr!" A few months later he woke us one spring morning at first light, calling intently—and repeatedly—from his room to announce what he could hear now that the storm windows had been removed: "Bird wake up!" We reinforce his enthusiasm, carrying Jacob to the window every night to say goodnight to his bird friends—and he learns something about what we value.

I love photographing the moon. Dory liked helping to watch for the moonrise, even at two years. Most faraway objects, however, cannot compete with small objects or organisms close at hand. In a child's landscape, everything reduces in scale. If we can be sufficiently patient, we adults can partake a little in our children's journey.

My children encounter various creatures outside our family, too. Dory returns home from a day at the babysitter asserting that, "Vampires are real; Michael says so." She plays with smiling plastic dinosaurs and My Little Ponies, watches Bambi, Benji, and Barney on video, and reads Dr. Seuss books—entering a sanitized world of happy anthropomorphs. Dory seems to distinguish between these play animals and real ones. She tells endless stories about her small realistic plastic animal figures. She asks to look at the bird book in the truck, leafs through *The Field Guide to Insects* in camp, and concludes that, "Insects don't know anything about love." She listens to fairy tales one night, National Geographic wildlife books the next, and then asks, not surprisingly: "Are wolves bad?"

Joanne and I take our children to the land in part because it simply feels good. Camping gives us a chance to be together without distractions, a place to play together. We also hope that a fundamental connection is growing from these experiences, that the earth will become a source of strength and sustenance for our children, a dependable spiritual bedrock. That feeling grows slowly; how can we nurture it? Experience, positive experience anywhere in the out-of-doors, seems the answer.

When Pueblo Indian potters speak of their work, and of passing on their knowledge to their children, over and over they speak of simply letting their children play with clay. The children learn by watching and doing, not by rote. Bernice Suazo-Naranjo, Taos Pueblo potter, learned potterymaking from her grandmother: "You've got to be there and do it; they are not going to explain, step by step."

As a child, potterymaking was simply part of what happened in Nora Naranjo-Morse's Santa Clara Pueblo home, along with cooking, eating, sleeping, and speaking the Tewa language. Now, she and her sisters and nieces make pottery, but, says Naranjo-Morse: "I rarely talk to my mother about pottery; that connection is instinctively there." Mother of twins on the verge of adolescence, Naranjo-Morse expressed her concern to me that: "A lot of Pueblo kids see this culture in a completely different perspective than our generation; they are more in touch with different worlds. That's why it's so important for me to keep talking to my kids. They don't understand the [Tewa] language; they just accept. And so we instill things in our kids that go beyond the language."

Pueblo Indian children learn about connections to the earth through virtually every experience in their culture. Beginning at about three years of age, Pueblo boys dance in their village plazas as animals, transforming themselves into the spirits of antelope and deer. They wear gray fox skins, deer-hoof and tortoise-shell rattles, parrot feathers, antler and horn headdresses, and skunk-fur gaiters. A little later, the girls may dance as parrots or buffalo mothers. The words of the songs, the symbols painted on costumes, and the choreographed gestures all connect the dancers with the earth: corn, clouds, the sun, rain, lightning, thunder, rainbows, evergreen trees. Life, growth, harvest.

Though I have watched Pueblo dances for many years, I can never share completely in Pueblo faith, even if that was my hope. I remain an outsider. But I feel reassured and renewed by these acts of ritual attention to the earth—to seasonal cycles and sacred mountains and nourishing rains. Pueblo dances remind me to pay more attention to my home landscape, to remember its power and the equality of all life.

And now I take my children to see the plaza dances. Through these occasional visits, I hope that they will come to respect the traditional Native American understanding of the earth and our relationship with its creatures. Pueblo Indian people generously share these ceremonies with anyone who comes to watch. By being there, respectfully, every spectator shares in the power of the dance, every person subtly increases the resonance of the connections celebrated by the dance.

I wonder how my children will remember these times. Dory's strongest memories so far include the snow cone given her by a corn dancer at San Felipe Pueblo and Nora Naranjo-Morse's family dogs, Snickers and Hamburger. Beyond these beginnings, what will my children's need for answers to mysteries lead them to believe? How will the land figure in our communal life?

They will come to know the canyons and mountains, and together we will watch for full moons and rainbows and mark each equinox and solstice. They will have a home landscape. They will not dance as animals or pray for rain to come to their clan's cornfield. They will likely learn more about other creatures from living with dogs and cats than from hunting deer or buffalo.

They will take in all we experience together and combine that with unique genetic destinies. These two forces together will carry them on their personal journeys. As parents, our job is to pay attention, to create possibilities—to be careful matchmakers between our children and the Earth.

S.T.

Notes

A Child's Sense of Wildness

3   Earlier versions of this essay—first written as a birthday gift to Caroline Wilson—have appeared in *Orion*, *Northern Lights*, *The Arizona Daily Star*, and in the anthology edited by Peter Sauer, *Finding Home* (Beacon Press, 1992).

I was first inspired to consider how exposure to the natural world affects child development by Edith Cobb's *The Ecology of Imagination in Childhood* (Columbia University Press, 1959) and Paul Shepard's *Nature and Madness* (Sierra Club Books, 1982). Jean Piaget's *The Child's Conception of the World* (Routledge and Kegan, 1929) and Robert Coles's *The Spiritual Life of Children* (Houghton Mifflin, 1990) are also important starting points regarding children's perceptions of their surroundings.

4   The quip on canyon country geomorphology is from Edward Abbey's *Desert Solitaire* (McGraw-Hill, 1968) and also accompanied a photo essay on "Arizona Territories" in the spring 1987 issue of *Wilderness* magazine, vol. 50, no. 177, p. 41.

7   Gaston Bachelard's ruminations about place and imagination are from *The Poetics of Space* (Beacon Press, 1964).

8   Mary Ann Kirby's "Nature as Refuge" essay includes many provocative observations about how small children use vegetation and semi-closed shelter. It appeared in *Children's Environments Quarterly* 6.1 (1989): 7–12.

9   Brian Sutton-Smith's "School Playground as Festival" also appeared in *Children's Environments Quarterly* 7.2 (1990): 3–7.

9   I wrote down the Franklin Burroughs quote when Burroughs, Trimble, Urmy, and I (among others) participated in a workshop on Cape Cod sponsored by the Orion Society, "The Undiscovered Country," in honor of John Hay in the fall of 1991.

11 Many of the statistics on demographic trends cited in this and other essays are from John McHale's *World Facts and Trends* (Collier Books, 1972); others are from the U.S. Department of Education hotline in Washington, D.C.

The Scripture of Maps, the Names of Trees

19   For the University of Pittsburgh analysis of cognitive maps, see "Stalking the Elusive Cognitive Map: The Development of Children's Representations of Geographic Space" in *Children and the Environment*, ed. Irwin Altman and Joachim F. Wohlwill (Plenum Press, 1978). Lynn S. Liben and Roger M. Downs's "Understanding Maps as Symbols: The Development of Map Concepts in Children" in *Advances in Child Development and Behavior*, vol. 22, ed. Hayne W. Reese (Academic Press, 1989), is exhaustive, literate, and clear.

20   Keith Basso's Apache landscape stories appear in "'Stalking with Stories': Names, Places, and Moral Narratives among the Western Apache" in his *Western Apache Language and Culture: Essays in Linguistic Anthropology* (University of Arizona Press, 1990).

22   Edith Cobb's classic essay, "The Ecology of Imagination in Childhood," appeared in *Daedalus* 88.3 (1959): 537–48; her book of the same title (Columbia University Press, 1977) expands her ideas.

23   The quote from Jean Baker Miller comes from her "The Development of Women's Sense of Self" (*Work in Progress* 12, The Stone Center, Wellesley College, 1984). *Your Child's Self-Esteem* (Doubleday/Dolphin, 1970), by Dorothy Corkille Briggs, details the classic challenges for parents who hope to give their children the power of self-esteem.

25   For more on "Nearby Nature," see Rachel and Stephen Kaplan's *The Experience of Nature: A Psychological Perspective* (Cambridge University Press, 1989).

26   In *An American Childhood* (Harper and Row, 1987), Annie Dillard wonderfully evokes the childhood of a kid obsessed with learning—especially learning about the natural world.

27   In *Childhood's Domain* (Croom-Helm, 1986), Robin C. Moore describes his field trips with children through their home territories in working-class British neighborhoods. His insights make good sense and are impressively rich with anecdotal detail.

27   The quote from Piaget is taken from Moore's *Childhood's Domain*.

27   Colin Ward, *The Child in the Country* (Robert Hale, 1988), corroborates Robin C. Moore's conclusions about the value of small places.

28   Melvin Konner's *Childhood* (Little, Brown, 1991) provides an elegantly written survey of the most recent research on child development, with care taken to include examples from many cultures.

28   Paul Shepard's "The Ark of the Mind" appeared in *Parabola* 8.2 (1983): 54–59.

Going Truant

35 Early versions of this essay, known as "The Evolution of a Naturalist," or "Finding the Wild Thread," appeared in *Petroglyph*, *The Land Report*, and the newsletter of the Burroughs Association, *Wake-Robin*. It was first presented orally as my acceptance speech for the Burroughs Medal in 1986.

39 Franklin Burroughs came up with the "going truant" quip at the fall 1991 "Undiscovered Country" colloquium in honor of his father-in-law, John Hay.

40 The poll data are paraphrased from conversations with Pew Memorial Trust staff involved with a Harris Poll of children's views of the environment, and a Voter Research & Surveys poll cited in *Newsweek* (November/December 1992, p. 10), in which the environment was lowest on the list of nine voters' concerns.

40 Peter Kalm's *Travels in America*, recounts 1750 (Dover, 1966).

40 Again, I am indebted to Paul Shepard's *Nature and Madness* (Sierra Club Books, 1982) for insights into mental and emotional development from an evolutionary perspective.

41 The 28 percent failure to complete high school is a statistic provided by the U.S. Department of Education's hotline.

41 VisionQuest information was provided by Bob and Clare Burton of VisionQuest National, P. O. Box 12906, Tucson, Arizona 85732. Their newsbrief, *Clarifier*, cites three independent evaluations which have determined that 69–86 percent of the juvenile delinquents with crime records who have participated in the VisionQuest programs have not been reincarcerated for any new crimes over the following years.

43 The Walkabout programs were featured in a special issue of the *Phi Delta Kappan* in May 1984. Among the articles included were founder Maurice Gibbons's "Walkabout Ten Years Later: Searching for a Renewed Vision of Education," pp. 591–600; and "The Rite of Passage for Walkabout," by Peter Copan and Eugene Lebwohl, pp. 602–3.

47 My paraphrasing of studies on hominid evolution draws heavily on Wendy Wilkins and Jennie Dunford's unpublished treatise called "Brain Evolution and the Emergence of Language Faculty" (Arizona State University Department of Literature and Languages, 1992); on Paul Shepard's *The Tender Carnivore and the Sacred Game* (Charles Scribner's Sons, 1973); and on Dorothy L. Cheney and Robert M. Seyfarth's *How Monkeys See the World* (University of Chicago Press, 1990). Brent Berlin's *Ethnobiological Classification* (Princeton University Press, 1992) has many insights regarding the

perceptual basis for hunter-gatherer societies' sense of order in the natural world. I am also indebted to the presentation on our predilection to savannas, made by Judith Heerwagen and Gordon H. Orians, "Humans, Habitability, Aesthetics," at the Woods Hole Oceanographic Institute symposium on biophilia; it is a chapter by the same name in the volume edited by Stephen R. Kellert and Edward O. Wilson, *The Biophilia Hypothesis* (Island Press, 1993), pp. 138–72.

A Land of One's Own

55   As in my other essays, I rely on Melvin Konner's *Childhood* (Little, Brown, 1991) for summaries of current research, in this case focusing on gender identity and sex roles. Jean Baker Miller, in *Toward a New Psychology of Women*, 2d ed. (Beacon Press, 1986), lays out the challenges of gender differences in American society, and her fine book is clearly central to my argument here. Carol Gilligan's more academic *In a Different Voice: Psychological Theory and Women's Development* (Harvard University Press, 1982) is another primary source. Mary Catherine Bateson's *Composing a Life* (Plume/Penguin, 1990) investigates the lives of professional American women balancing professions with relationships and family. Carolyn Heilbrun's *Writing a Woman's Life* (Norton, 1988) eloquently shows how constrained women's stories have been and clearly lays out a future of extraordinary possibilities.

57   Marcia Bonta's *Women in the Field: America's Pioneering Women Naturalists* (Texas A&M University Press, 1991) nicely fills a historical gap. The best resource for women's natural history writing is Lorraine Anderson's *Sisters of the Earth: Women's Prose and Poetry about Nature* (Vintage, 1991). Thomas J. Lyon's *This Incomperable Lande: A Book of American Nature Writing* (Houghton Mifflin, 1989) also is a fine book. See my introduction to *Words from the Land: Encounters with Natural History Writing* (Gibbs Smith, 1989) for further thoughts about gender and the psychology of nature writing.

57   My comments about Rachel Carson are based on Paul Brooks, *Speaking For Nature* (Sierra Club Books, 1980).

61   See Teresa Jordan, *Cowgirls: Women of the American West* (Anchor Press, 1982), for the best source for life histories of ranch women. Her memoir, *Riding the White Horse Home: A Western Family Album* (Pantheon, 1993), is a lovely portrait of her own ranch childhood and includes many observations relevant to gender issues.

62   Leslie Ryan's strong essay, "The Clearing in the Clearing," begins with pondering being alone in the land and moves to the connec-

tion between rape of women and the rape of the land (*Northern Lights* 8.3 [Fall 1992]: 27–30). See Marcia Bonta's piece, "Coming Home," in *On Nature's Terms*, ed. Thomas J. Lyon and Peter Stine (Texas A&M University Press, 1992).

66   Robin C. Moore summarized his research in "The Power of Nature Orientations of Girls and Boys Toward Biotic and Abiotic Play Settings on a Reconstructed Schoolyard," *Children's Environments Quarterly* 3.3 (Fall 1986): 52–69.

67   Research on unequal treatment in the classroom is summarized in Jean Wollam, "The Advantage of Same-Sex Programs," *The Gifted Child Today* (March/April 1990): 22–24, and "Women in Science and Environmental Education: Need for an Agenda," by Kristin Benne Kremer, Gary W. Mullins, and Robert E. Roth, *Journal of Environmental Education* 22.2 (1990): 4–6.

71   See the excellent *Children's Experience of Place* by Roger Hart (Irvington Publishers, 1979) and "The Development of Environmental Competence in Girls and Boys," by Susan Saegert and Roger Hart, in *Play: Anthropological Perspectives*, ed. Michael A. Salter (Leisure Press, 1978).

72   M. H. Matthews, *Making Sense of Place: Children's Understanding of Large-Scale Environments* (Harvester Wheatsheaf/Barnes and Noble, 1992), provides a useful current summary of research on spatial skills.

73   For women on the American frontier, see Annette Kolodny, *The Land Before Her: Fantasy and Experience of the American Frontiers, 1630–1860* (University of North Carolina Press, 1984).

73   Sherry B. Ortner outlines our cultural stereotypes in "Is Female to Male as Nature Is to Culture?" in *Woman, Culture, and Society*, ed. Michelle Z. Rosaldo and Louse Lamphere (Stanford University Press, 1974). Susan Griffin's remarkable *Woman and Nature: The Roaring Inside Her* (Harper and Row, 1978) is enlightening and harrowing.

Children in Touch, Creatures in Story

79   My interest in learning how children in traditional societies learn about the natural world was inspired by David Orr's fine work in conservation education, including his book of essays, *Ecological Literacy* (State University of New York Press, 1992). Richard Nelson was the first to express to me that at the heart of each native culture's ethnobiological knowledge is the teaching to their children of hundreds of rules about appropriate responses to local plants and animals. For a sense of such a traditional framework of ecological ethics, see his *Make Prayers to the Raven* (University of

Chicago Press, 1985), and his chapter, "Searching for the Lost Arrow: Physical and Spiritual Ecology in the Hunter's World," in *The Biophilia Hypothesis*, ed. Stephen R. Kellert and Edward O. Wilson (Island Press, 1993), pp. 201–28.

83   Leslie Marmon Silko's fine essay, "Landscape, History, and the Pueblo Imagination," has been reprinted in several books, including Daniel Halpern's edited volume, *On Nature* (North Point Press, 1987). Martha Monroe has recently demonstrated that narrative stories are not only more interesting to students than conventional science texts, but that this interest is correlated positively with increased knowledge and activism. I refer to her 1991–1992 effort presented orally at environmental education conferences, "Alternatives to Traditional Text in the Communication of Environmental Information," a currently unpublished study, c/o Martha Monroe, 7127 Maple Ave., Takoma Park, Maryland 20912.

84   Although much of my focus here is on what adults traditionally teach children, David S. Sutherland and Sam H. Ham have recently investigated information flowing the other direction; see their "Child-to-Parent Transfer of Environmental Ideology in Costa Rican Families: An Ethnographic Case Study," *Journal of Environmental Education* 23.3 (1992): 9–16.

86   Robert Michael Pyle has spoken and written on the loss of experiential knowledge of nature in several settings, including "Intimate Relations and the Extinction of Experience," *Left Bank* 2 (1992): 61–69, also to be included in a book of essays called *The Thunder Tree* (Houghton Mifflin, 1993).

86   Much of my discussion of Yaqui, O'odham, Anglo, and Hispanic children in the desert is derived from a summer 1992 study which I collaborated on with Sara St. Antoine of the Yale School of Forestry and Environmental Studies, with assistance from the Pew Scholars Program and the Arizona-Sonora Desert Museum Education Department. Another, more technical version of our results was presented at a workshop in August 1992 at Woods Hole Oceanographic Institute and is included in Kellert and Wilson's *The Biophilia Hypothesis*, as "The Loss of Floral and Faunal Story: The Extinction of Experience," pp. 229–50. See also *Buzzworm* 4.2 (July/August 1992): 88.

87   Among Stephen Kellert's many contributions to the sociology of environmental perception is his pioneering work in collaboration with Miriam Westervelt, *Children's Attitudes, Knowledge, and Behaviors Toward Animals* (U.S. Department of Interior, Fish and Wildlife Service, 1983).

88   Jerry Mander interviewed Lennie, Smith, and other Native Americans about the impacts of the media on their traditions for his book, *In the Absence of the Sacred* (Sierra Club Books, 1991).

89 For a review of Inuit vision and myopia, see the several references discussed by George C. Williams and Randolph M. Nesse, "The Dawn of Darwinian Medicine," *Quarterly Review of Biology* 66 (1991): 1–21. See also Edmund C. Carpenter, *Eskimo Realities* (Holt, Rinehart and Winston, 1974), and Barry Lopez's *Arctic Dreams* (Charles Scribner's Sons, 1986).

90 The comment by paleoecologist David Steadman—a friend from graduate school days—is paraphrased from a public television interview with him regarding his early motivations toward nature study, included in a special program regarding his reconstruction of Galápagos finch phylogeny.

92 Rosilda Manuel, current Education Director for the Tohono O'odham Reservation, made these comments to me in relation to her participation in the Prescott College Master's Degree Program, regarding her changing perception of the relationship between cultural and environmental education strategies.

93 Felipe C. Molina, Yaqui poet and singer, has collaborated with Larry Evers on a remarkable study of the Yoeme view of the wilderness world, *Yaqui Deer Songs: Maso Bwikam* (University of Arizona Press, 1987).

94 The quote from Italo Calvino comes from his fine novel, *Mr. Palomar*, translated into English by William Weaver (New York: Harcourt, Brace and Jovanovich, 1983).

94 The loss of native languages has been eloquently placed into perspective by Richard and Nora Marks Dauenhauer, "Native Language Survival," *Left Bank* 2 (1992): 115–22. It is also estimated that at least half of the world's extant six thousand languages will disappear over the next hundred years.

98 Aaron Katcher and Gregory Wilkins's discussion of nature as therapy appears as "Dialogue with Animals—Its Nature and Culture," in Kellert and Wilson's *The Biophilia Hypothesis*, pp. 173–99.

99 I interviewed Peggy Turk-Boyer, Director of the Centro para Estudios de los Desiertos y Oceanos (CEDO), at her home in Puerto Penasco, Mexico. For further information, see *CEDO News*, obtained from CEDO, 2601 Airport Rd., Tucson, Arizona 85706.

100 Johnny Moses is quoted in Brenda Peterson's essay, "Animals as Brothers and Sisters," in Thomas J. Lyon's anthology, *On Nature's Terms* (Texas A&M University Press, 1992).

100 Kamau Kambui and I both participated in a Wilder Forest conference, "Children, Youth and the Future of Wilderness," in a cross-cultural perspective, in October of 1989. Our mutual friend, Jim Mason, Wilder Forest Director, graciously gathered various press clippings and Wilder Forest pamphlets about Kambui and the Underground Railroad for me, including the anonymous "Reenactment Deals with Realism," from *Wilder News*, July 1992, p. 1; and

Charles L. Blockson's "The Underground Railroad," *National Geographic* 166.1 (1984): 3–40. For further information, write Underground Railroad, Wilder Forest, Ostlund Trail, Marine-on-St. Croix, Minnesota 55047. For more discussion of environmental education's historic failure to appeal to many people of color, see Larry M. Gigliotti's article, "Environmental Education: What Went Wrong? What Can Be Done?" in *Journal of Environmental Education* 22.1 (1991): 9–12.

102   Daniel Pablo's story was offered by him to a group of forty-three Native American farmers and gardeners 10–12 July 1992 in Gallup, New Mexico; it was later published as "Daniel's Story," in 1992 issues of *Traditional Farming Today* and *The Seedhead News*, both occasional publications of Native Seeds/Search, 2509 North Campbell Avenue, No. 325, Tucson, Arizona 85719. Daniel has been a friend of mine since age four, and so I was grateful to accompany him, his grandmother, and grandfather to the farmers' conference.

106   The field interview with Laura Kerman occurred in Topawa, Arizona, between 1982 and 1984, and was shown on a Phoenix television show.

A Wilderness, with Cows

112   Statistics about children in developing countries can be found in *When the Bough Breaks: Our Children, Our Environment* by Lloyd Timberlake and Laura Thomas (Earthscan Publications, 1990).

112   Joseph G. Jorgensen's perspectives always make interesting reading; see "Land Is Cultural, So Is a Commodity: The Locus of Differences Among Indians, Cowboys, Sod-Busters, and Environmentalists," *The Journal of Ethnic Studies* 12.3 (1984): 1–21. James Garbarino, "Habitats for Children: An Ecological Perspective," is also useful; it appears in *Habitats for Children: The Impacts of Density*, ed. Joachim F. Wohlwill and Willem van Vliet (Lawrence Erlbaum Associates, 1985).

113   Historical perspective on the United States comes from *Growing Up with the Country: Childhood on the Far Western Frontier* by Elliott West (University of New Mexico Press, 1989).

117   Elko ranked first in Norman Crampton's *The 100 Best Small Towns in America* (Prentice Hall, 1993).

121   Wallace Stegner, who understood the West better than anyone, distilled his knowledge in his last book, *Where the Bluebird Sings to the Lemonade Springs: Living and Writing in the West* (Random House, 1992), from which my quotes come.

123   Results of the 1992 survey of children's sources of environmental information appeared in *Buzzworm* 4.2 (July/August 1992): 88.

123 Camp Timanous is in Raymond, Maine, and my quotes come from their 1993 catalog.

124 Jim Carrier's *West of the Divide: Voices From a Ranch and a Reservation* (Fulcrum, 1992) is a fine book that vividly and truly evokes the daily life of a ranch family (and a Ute Mountain Ute family, as well).

124 See Teresa Jordan's works listed in the notes to chap. 4 ("A Land of One's Own") as well as "Beyond Conflict" in *Dry Crik Review* (Spring 1992) and "Ranch Family" in *Ranching Traditions: Legacy of the American West* (Abbeville Press, 1989).

125 Robert Coles has charted most of the territory in this book before us; see, especially, *The Spiritual Life of Children* (Houghton Mifflin, 1990).

128 L. Jackson Newell provides the best source about Deep Springs in "Among the Few at Deep Springs College: Assessing a Seven-Decade Experiment in Liberal Education," *The Journal of General Education* 34.2 (1982): 120–34.

129 See Rachel and Stephen Kaplan's *The Experience of Nature: A Psychological Perspective* (Cambridge University Press, 1989) for detailed results from their Michigan study.

130 For a controversial philosophy of natural resource management, see the publications of the Center for Holistic Resource Management (HRM), Albuquerque, New Mexico, and Allan Savory's *Holistic Resource Management* (Island Press, 1988). The fall 1992 issue of the HRM newsletter (no. 37: "Healing the Public Lands") offers a good summary of Savory's ideas and the emotional reactions they provoke.

131 The quote from William Kittredge comes from *Hole in the Sky: A Memoir* (Alfred A. Knopf, 1992).

132 Linda Hasselstrom ponders many of the ideas in this essay in her fine *Land Circle: Writings Collected from the Land* (Fulcrum, 1991). See, especially, the title essay. To keep in touch with the ongoing discussion about ranching's future in the West, read *High Country News* (Paonia, Colorado), the West's biweekly environmental newspaper and a clearinghouse for thoughtful people spread across many hundreds of miles who nonetheless comprise a community. Editorials by *HCN* editor Ed Marston influence my thinking here.

Learning Herps

136 Edward O. Wilson's *Biophilia* (Harvard University Press, 1984) discusses snake phobia (and why it is a form of biophilia) in a preliminary way; he extends the discussion in the essay, "Biophilia

and the Conservation Ethic," his chapter in the anthology he has edited with Stephen Kellert, *The Biophilia Hypothesis* (Island Press, 1993), pp. 31–41. Wilson draws heavily on the ideas of Bajaji Mundkur's *The Cult of the Serpent: An Interdisciplinary View of Its Manifestations and Origins* (State University of New York Press, 1983).

141   Stephen Kellert and Joyce Berry discuss the American disdain for herps and insects in "Phase III: Knowledge, Affection and Basic Attitudes towards Animals in American Society," a 1980 report to the U.S. Fish and Wildlife Service; while dogs, horses, and swans are tops in popularity polls, cockroaches, mosquitos, rats, wasps, rattlesnakes are the pits; lizards and frogs are also low on the preference scale. Kellert summarized some of the same data in "Attitudes towards Animals: Age-Related Development among Children," *Journal of Environmental Education* 16.3 (1985): 129–35.

147   To look at specific interactions between people and herps, there are several excellent case studies. See Wade Sherbrooke's *Horned Lizards of Southwestern North America* (Southwest Parks and Monuments Association, 1981), and Dennis Cornejo's "Night of the Spadefoot Toad," in *Science* 82 (1982): 62–65.

151   Donald Bahr, Juan Gregorio, David Lopez, and Albert Alvarez discuss horned lizard sickness in *Piman Shamanism and Staying Sickness (Ka:cim Mumkidag)* (University of Arizona Press, 1975).

154   Lynn Margulis and Dorion Sagan devote an entire chapter, "Lizard Twists," to vestiges of reptilian sexuality in human behavior in their recent book, *Mystery Dance: On the Evolution of Human Sexuality* (Summit Books, 1991).